Table of Contents

ACRONYMNS

ANC	Armeé National Congolaise
BiH	Army of the Republic of Bosnia and Herzegovina
BSA	Bosnian Serb Army
C2	Command and Control
HVO	Croatian Defense Council
JNA	Yugoslav People's Army
NATO	North Atlantic Treaty Organization
ONUC	United Nations Operations in the Congo
UN	United Nations
UNF	United Nations Force
UNPROFOR	United Nations Protection Force
UNSC	United Nations Security Council
UNSCR	United Nations Security Council Resolution
US	United States

Introduction

To our friends and allies, the Libyan intervention demonstrates what the international community can achieve when we stand together as one—although the efforts in Libya are not yet over. NATO has once more proven that it is the most capable alliance in the world and that its strength comes from both its firepower and the power of our democratic ideals. And the Arab members of our coalition have stepped up and shown what can be achieved when we act together as equal partners. Their actions send a powerful message about the unity of our effort and our support for the future of Libya.[1]

— President Barack Obama

If you concentrate exclusively on victory, with no thought for the after effect, you may be too exhausted to profit by the peace, while it is almost certain that the peace will be a bad one, containing the germs of another war. This is a lesson supported by abundant experience. The risks become greater still in any war that is waged by a coalition, or in such a case a too complete victory inevitably complicates the problem of making a just and wise peace settlement. Where there is no longer the counterbalance of an opposing force to control the appetites between the parties to the alliance. The divergence is then apt to become so acute as to turn the comradeship of common danger into the hostility of mutual dissatisfaction—so that the ally of one war becomes the enemy in the next.[2]

— B.H. Liddell Hart

Governments form military coalitions to pursue their common interests and shared policy objectives. There are numerous advantages to this collective approach with respect to world and regional politics. However executing military operations by committee is fraught with additional inefficiencies and friction. Does fighting as a coalition reduce the likelihood of attaining success due to the hazard of a lack of unity of command?

This topic is important for numerous reasons the foremost of which, is the fact that the United States (US) is currently and will continue to participate in military operations as part of a coalition for the foreseeable future. Additionally the principle of unity of command is widely accepted as true yet there has been very little research done on how coalition warfare affects unity

---

[1]White House, "Statement by the President on Libya," August 22, 2011, http://www.whitehouse.gov/the-press-office/2011/08/22/statement-president-libya (accessed June 12, 2012).

[2]B. H. Liddell Hart, *Strategy* (New York: Praeger, 1954), 366.

1

of command, cause friction, or impacts the odds of mission success. The character and composition of an intervention force has gotten scant attention. While much work has been done on why and when states intervene and the likelihood of success, surprising little research has been done on how the nature of a coalition impacts the outcome of the conflict. What risk is assumed by choosing to fight as a coalition? Only by properly examining the risk associated with coalitions can we hope to mitigate them and maximize the opportunities available to us through partnering.

While coalitions are often beneficial with respect to international politics, multinational operations are often detrimental to the military campaign at the local level. The two greatest externalities of coalition warfare are the negative impacts on the ability to make decisions and resourcing issues. Fighting as coalition increases friction at the theater and tactical level making it harder for commanders to achieve the strategic aims envisioned by their political leaders. Stated another way, rallying others to the cause may actually limit action and effectiveness.

All things being equal, we must assume that intervening as a unitary actor is more efficient and has a greater likelihood of achieving its operational objectives. A single actor does not need to spend time and energy building consensus around decisions. When a state fights alone it can focus on its own national strategy and is accountable only to its own constituents. Additionally, more resources are available and all of a state's sources of power are potentially available. While the state must often justify its employment decisions, rarely do leaders ask permission to use military power. So why form coalitions? The motivation to form coalitions can be understood in various ways to include geopolitics, resources, and obligations.

Waging war as a coalition may protect political capital and even increase it, whereas acting unilaterally can expose a state to international criticism and accusations of aggression. States do risk their political capital when choosing to wage war or intervene militarily. Being perceived favorably plays out on various levels from local politics and domestic audiences, worldwide public opinion, to relations with other states and international governmental

2

organizations such as the United Nations (UN). When choosing to act or not, each state weighs the rewards and risks to themselves with respect to their political capital.

States are often motivated to form coalitions even when they have sufficient military capacity to reduce the amount of risk they face. Instead of a state committing a large portion of its own forces, it may seek another state to contribute troops. This substitution allows each state to have more forces uncommitted and available to respond to other situations should the need arise. Thus, the pooling of resources has reduced each state's overall security risk by keeping more of its own force available for contingencies.

Sometimes states fight as part of a combined force because of their obligations. The obligations may be either direct or indirect and come from various sources. Being part of a security alliance can directly lead one state to contribute forces to a combined fight. This occurred when the North Atlantic Treaty Organization (NATO) invoked Article 5 of their treaty following the attacks on 9-11, stating that the attack against the US was an attack against all members of the alliance. Additionally, being a member of the UN also entails its own set of obligations, albeit they are generally viewed as weaker. For example, in the 2005 World Summit Outcome, the UN General Assembly unanimously adopted the principle of the responsibility to protect, which states that members and the international community through the UN have a responsibility to protect populations from genocide, war crimes, ethnic cleansing, and crimes against humanity.[3] While all member states acknowledge their responsibility to protect, this agreement does not trigger rapid military responses the way a collective security alliance would.

Research questions: Does intervening on the side of the government increase the government's odds of winning? Additionally does fighting as a multinational force affect the likelihood of success in military interventions, on the side of the government?

---

[3]United Nations, General Assembly, A/RES/60/1, *2005 World Summit Outcome*, 60th Sess., http://www.un.org/summit2005/ (accessed November 14, 2012), 30, para. 138-139.

This research question contains numerous key terms and concepts that are worth defining since they are applicable throughout. The literature review contains additional key concepts. In analyzing coalition warfare it is important that we define and differentiate between certain terms.

The term coalition has various meanings and is often used in different senses. Coalition warfare is often loosely used to describe any instance where one side is comprised of more than one state. This definition is too broad and allows the terms coalitions and alliances to be conflated and used interchangeably. For the purposes of this paper a coalition is a military force formed ad hoc to address a particular situation, threat, or enemy. An alliance is a pre established collective security agreement. An alliance often has many organizational advantages and efficiencies over a coalition gained through a shared hierarchy, doctrine, interoperability of equipment, and previous collective training. NATO is a good illustration of a security alliance that contains each of the above advantages. A coalition can be built around a standing alliance when additional states contribute assets to a combined fight. An example of this is the NATO led International Security Assistance Force in Afghanistan.

Within the US Army the term stability operations is clearly defined and widely understood. Army doctrine states that: "Stability operations are military missions, tasks, and activities conducted outside the United States to maintain or reestablish a safe and secure environment and to provide essential governmental services, emergency infrastructure reconstruction, and humanitarian relief. They include five tasks: establish civil security, establish civil control, restore essential services, support to governance, and support to economic and infrastructure development."[4]

---

[4]Department of the Army, ADP 3-0, *Unified Land Operations* (Washington, DC: Government Printing Office, October 2011), 6.

Patrick Regan's work provides a useful definition of a successful military intervention in an internal conflict, as stopping the fighting and stability in the region.[5] Politicians often decide to intervene for a complex range of reasons and interests, yet stopping the fighting and stability in the region are a common thread, generally present as policy goals.[6] This definition is also sufficiently abstract to facilitate quantitative and qualitative comparisons across a diverse range of military interventions.

The structure of this monograph is literature review, methodology, followed by case studies of the Congo Civil War and Bosnia, and a conclusion. This monograph uses a combination of quantitative and qualitative analysis. The literature review will critically examine the preceding body of work on military interventions both in general and coalitions to inform the case studies. The methodology section details the quantitative analysis and case study selection. The conclusion summarizes the findings and implications and recommends topics for further research.

---

[5]Patrick Regan, *Civil Wars and Foreign Powers: Outside Intervention in Intrastate Conflict* (Ann Arbor, MI: University of Michigan Press, 2002), ix.

[6]Ibid.

Literature Review

And we will pursue engagement with hostile nations to test their intentions, give their governments the opportunity to change course, reach out to their people, and mobilize international coalitions.

— White House, *National Security Strategy*

The following literature review provides historic context and a critical analysis of the more relevant academic works related to military interventions in internal conflicts. This review will begin by looking at the literature on conflict outcomes and competing definitions of success, to enable examination of the ability of multinational coalitions to influence the outcome in favor of the government. The research questions, "does intervening on the side of the government increase their odds of winning and does fighting as a multinational force affect the likelihood of success in military interventions?" implies three main components, how are the resources are organized, the concept of success, and amount of resources available. The literature review mirrors the research question and will further refine and examine these variables and concludes with a list of variables generated from the literature review.

The US has and will continue to participate in military operations across the spectrum of conflict as part of a coalition. For almost half of the 20th century security alliances, not coalitions, dominated the collective security landscape with the formation of NATO and the Warsaw Pact in 1949 and 1955 respectively. The dissolution of the USSR in 1991 greatly changed the international security environment and corresponding theory.

The fall of the Warsaw Pact resulted in renewed interested in coalition warfare.[7] Many analysts predicted that the end of Cold War would produce a peace dividend. Unfortunately, these predictions were incorrect. In fact, the number of wars actually continued to increase. James

---

[7]Anthony J. Rice, "Command and Control: The Essence of Coalition Warfare," *Parameters* (Spring 1997): 152.

6

Fearon and David Laitin's research of civil wars from 1945 to 1999 demonstrates an increasing accumulation of civil wars with an outbreak rate of 2.31 per year outpacing the resolution rate of 1.85 per year. While not seemingly contributing to an increase in war, the end of the Cold War allowed states to intervene without accidently causing a nuclear world war. Coalitions were formed to liberate Kuwait, conduct peacekeeping operations in the Balkans, and to combat Islamic extremist terrorist organizations. Military coalitions became the norm whereas alliances and unilateral actions became the exception. The end of the Cold War created the conditions that allowed states to use their militaries abroad to a much greater extent, and many of them did. While later research by John Mueller has shown that the incidents of war have now greatly declined, and argues that the norms against war have strengthened.[8] Despite these trends in the amount of wars being waged, political rhetoric still stresses that the US plans to employ its military as part of a multinational operation.

While partnering has become the norm it is unclear whether coalition warfare is the most effective way to fight. The international community, often through the forum of the UN, has greatly improved their ability to build consensus to authorize military options. Political leaders and diplomats have also proven adept at forming the coalitions necessary to carry out these approved military missions. The forming of coalitions makes perfect sense with respect to geopolitics. Many countries, including the US, plan to fight as coalition or alliance as a means of mitigating their own risk as they reduce their own forces and defense budgets. The Department of Defense recently described partnering as a means of economizing force when it announced its plan to "develop innovative, low-cost, and small-footprint approaches to achieve our security objectives, relying on exercises, rotational presence, and advisory capabilities"[9] Some of the ways

---

[8]John Mueller, "War Has Almost Ceased to Exist: An Assessment," *Political Science Quarterly* 124 (November 2009): 297-321.

[9]Department of Defense, *Defense Budget Priorities and Choices* (Washington, DC: Government Printing Office, 2012), 6.

and means listed include the Global Security Contingency Fund and the Security Force Assistance Program.[10] Simply put, international consensus and the resultant coalitions allow states to conduct more military operations, be they interventions or war. Yet, are coalitions the best means to fight a war? How does coalition warfare increase risk and friction at the operational and tactical levels of war?

Regardless of whether coalition warfare is the most effective means militarily, many believe it will be the norm. Then General Robert RisCassi was an early advocate and thinker with respect to the need to develop a doctrine of coalition warfare. He argues that the trend of fighting as a coalition would continue and that necessitated a corresponding coalition doctrine.[11] He argues that a coalition needs "a common doctrine to take advantage of commonalties."[12] He highlights that doctrine is not simply how a force fights, but also how it communicates, and understands the situation. He then proposes four tenets largely derived from the principles of war to serve as the foundation of a coalition doctrine. These tenets are agility, initiative, depth, and synchronization.[13] After describing why we need a coalition doctrine and what should it contain, he address a framework for planning coalition operations.

His logic for planning, organizing, and leading coalition operations is linear, logically sound, and accounts for the various levels of war. Planning begins from shared coalition national interests and objectives. The shared coalition doctrine enables the development of a coalition strategy and supporting campaign, which synchronizes all the elements of combat power and tactical actions. This nearly parallels the concepts of unity of effort and operational art found in current Army doctrine.

---

[10]Ibid.

[11]Robert W. RisCassi, "Principles for Coalition Warfare," *Joint Forces Quarterly* (Summer 1993): 58-71.

[12]Ibid., 60.

[13]Ibid.

While RisCassi's work was vital to the evolution of combined doctrine, there are some internal contradictions and issues contained in it. RisCassi focuses on standing coalitions with the development and organization of ad hoc coalitions receiving limited attention. He was probably influenced by the fact that he was serving as the Commander in Chief of the UN and Republic of Korea-US Combined Forces Command at the time of publication. Furthermore, he repeatedly conflates the terms coalition with security alliance. While both are forms of combined warfare, they are not the same. Many of his prescriptions, i.e. common doctrine and collective training, are more feasible within a standing alliance than an ad hoc coalition. The above issues result in a slightly idealized understanding of feasibility of developing common doctrine, strategy, and campaigns within a coalition.

RisCassi also failed to identify and resolve the fact there is significant tension between two of his main tenets. The tenets of initiative and synchronization are contradictory and inherently at odds with one another. Synchronization requires thorough planning and coordination. However, while discussing initiative he highlights that the more detailed and inhibiting, a plan may limit or restrain initiative. He does not truly highlight or propose to resolve this tension. Tension is irresolvable. However, his article is useful in many ways in that it spurred professional thinking and dialogue, provided a broad conceptual framework, and illustrates historic dialogue and evolution of joint doctrine with respect to coalition warfare.

It seems nearly impossible to have any dialogue reference Joint Interagency Intergovernmental Multinational, without using the terms unity of command and unity of effort. The importance and validity of these concepts is seemingly unquestioned even though many are unfamiliar with their genesis. The principles of war serve as part of the enduring theoretical foundation of warfare. The US and other nations later refined and codified their own version of the principles of war. Since 1947, US joint doctrine has included nine principles of war. They are objective, offensive, mass, maneuver, economy of force, unity of command, security, surprise, and simplicity.[14] The current version of Joint Publication 3-0, *Joint Operations* adds three additional principles, restraint, perseverance, and legitimacy, deduced from US military experiences.[15]

Understanding the definition, importance, central role, that unity of command plays in joint operations, supports further examining and including it as an independent variable. Various forms of the intervening forces and command structure affect the corresponding level of unity of command. The fewer decision makers that are present, the easier it is to maintain unity of command. The following list details possible forms the stability force can take in descending orders. When a country intervenes unilaterally or conducts stability operations by themselves in their own country, there is unity of command. When one country intervenes at the request of the host nation, there is often a unity of effort with the two countries working in concert. Next in the descending order is an intervention by a standing security alliance, i.e. NATO. Coalitions can be divided into those organized by Inter Governmental Organizations and those without any preexisting structure. Either form of coalition can have a lead nation or parallel structure.

Related and increasingly emphasized concepts are that of unity of action and effort. Current US joint doctrine defines unity of action as "(t)he synchronization, coordination, and/or integration of the activities of governmental and nongovernmental entities with military operations to achieve unity of effort."[16] This is also commonly referred to as a whole of government approach. Doctrine defines unity of effort as the "(c)oordination and cooperation

---

[14]Joint Chiefs of Staff, Joint Publication (JP) 3-0, *Joint Operations* (Washington, DC: Government Printing Office, 2011), 1-2.

[15]Ibid.

[16]Joint Chiefs of Staff, Joint Publication (JP) 1-0, *Joint Personnel Support* (Washington, DC: Government Printing Office, 2011).

toward common objectives, even if the participants are not necessarily part of the same command or organization-the product of successful unified action."[17]

US joint doctrine has three types of organizational structure for command and control during multinational operations. They are integrated, lead nation, and parallel. An integrated command has a single commander, with the attendant headquarters, and subordinate commanders also being integrated and multinational down to the lowest echelon practicable.[18] The lead nation command structure places all member nations' forces under the control of one nation.[19] This structure is often characterized by the lead nation providing the headquarters, to include both the command and staff elements with the subordinate commands retaining national integrity. Parallel command is the last basic type of multinational command structure and is characterized by the lack of a single force commander.[20] Since there is no shared commander or headquarters, coalition leadership must establish a way to coordinate their actions, such as a coordination center.[21]

The multinational forces doctrine makes some additional key points that illustrate some of the nuances that occur when multinational forces are organized in practice. The first is that regardless of the structure, each troop contributing nation often establishes its own national command element, outside of the multinational command structure, to exercise its own responsibility for its forces and aid in administration.[22] Additionally different types of

---

[17]Ibid.

[18]Joint Chiefs of Staff, Joint Publication (JP) 3-16, *Multinational Operations* (Washington, DC: Government Printing Office, 2007), II-6.

[19]Ibid.

[20]Ibid., II-7.

[21]Ibid.

[22]Ibid.

organizations tend to use particular command structures. Alliances tend to use integrated or lead nation structures, whereas coalitions often use either lead nation or parallel commands.[23]

It is necessary to understand the literature on why interventions are successful before examining the specifics of multinational interventions. Numerous well known and esteemed authors have contributed greatly to the body of work relating to civil wars, peace operations, counterinsurgency, and the like. The literature on military interventions is vast and offers various ways to evaluate missions as successful. Literature discusses the theory of the role of military power in international relations and intrastate wars, why states intervene, the various approaches to intervention, theory of how military interventions can be used to affect outcomes, and various means of measuring and evaluating interventions. The literature tends to focus on either the idealistic goals of intervention or the political goals sought by governments that choose to intervene. However, idealism and politics are not distinctly bifurcated. While idealism often influences the political goals sought, the policy aims may be purely interest driven.

J. David Singer's work on how nations influence each other is still influential to the logic of military interventions and widely cited in the literature.[24] Singer argues that there are three major dimensions of inter-nation influence which inform how an influencer sets out to influence another state's future action. They are perceived behavior, predicted behavior, and preferred behavior.[25] He goes on to state that the two techniques available to the influencer are threat and promise.[26] Threat goes with punishment while promise goes with reward.[27] He argues that reward power often requires the expenditure of enormous amounts of resources to have the desired effect

---

[23]Ibid., II-9.

[24]J. David Singer, "Inter-nation Influence: A Formal Model," *The American Political Science Review* 57, no. 2 (June 1963): 420-430.

[25]Ibid., 423.

[26]Ibid., 426-427.

[27]Ibid., 427.

12

and that due to the non-hierarchical, international anarchy, coercive power is often the only feasible way to influence. However, the ability to influence through threats is limited.[28] For example, the threatened state may not concede in the short-term due to their estimate that the precedent of concession will result in their receiving more threats.[29]

Thomas Schelling's "The Diplomacy of Violence" argues that while military strategy used to be thought of as the science for victory, this is no longer true. Military strategy now includes the art of coercion, intimidation, and deterrence with serving a punitive role.[30] "Military strategy, whether we like it or not, has become the diplomacy of violence,"[31] Like Singer, Schelling's theory about interstate relations is also useful in explaining and understanding why states intervene and how actors behave in intrastate wars. Both Singer and Schelling can be used to argue that the way to evaluate whether an intervention was successful was whether it was able to cause the preferred behavior, or has the threat or use of force coerced the belligerents to behavior as the interveners wanted.

Stathis Kalyvas also applies and expands upon the concepts of Singer and Schelling in his development of theory of irregular war as it relates to the ability to control people and cause collaboration.[32] He argues that military resources generally override the population's pre-war political and social preferences. However, he continues that it often requires enormous military resources to assert permanent control in a country, in civil war. There are usually not enough military resources to overwhelm the population of a country numerically and to deter it by presence. This necessitates the need to effectively use the military resources available to include

---

[28]Ibid., 428.

[29]Ibid., 430.

[30]Thomas C. Shelling, *Arms and Influence* (New Haven: Yale University Press, 1966) Chapter 1.

[31]Ibid.

[32]Stathis N. Kalyvas, *The Logic of Violence in Civil Wars* (Cambridge: Cambridge University Press, 2006), Chapter 5.

the discriminate use of violence. Kalyvas argues that violence is used as an instrument to generate collaboration or deterrence. He then differentiates between selective and indiscriminate violence in civil war. The difference between the two types is that selective violence "entails personal targeting" whereas indiscriminate implies collective targeting.[33] He argues that the use of selective violence is a key instrument for generating and maintaining control, it generates collaboration and deters defection to the rival camp but indiscriminate violence is of limited value and often counterproductive.[34]

The idea of success in military interventions and war in general has evolved over time. An early and oft cited theorist is Paul Diehl who proposes two criteria for evaluating interventions in his book, *International Peacekeeping*. The first is limiting the fighting while the second is promoting conflict resolution. This is similar to Regan's success criteria, of stopping the fighting between groups and regional stability.[35]

Since competing claims to sovereignty lies at the heart of civil war, then the presence of divided sovereignty is another way to measure the affect of military intervention. Kalyvas argues that at its core lies the breakdown of the monopoly of violence, by way of territorial based armed challenge and that divides the terrain into the categories of incumbent controlled, insurgent controlled, and zones of contested control.[36] Licklider argues that a civil war is over when there are no longer multiple claims to sovereignty and the absence of fighting for five years.[37] Both Kalyvas's and Licklider's discussion of divided sovereignty and control are useful in analyzing and measuring results in civil war.

---

[33]Ibid., 142.

[34]Ibid, 141-145.

[35]Regan, Chapter 1.

[36]Kalyvas, 88.

[37]Roy Licklider, ed., *Stop the Killing: How Civil Wars End* (New York: New York University Press, 1993).

Robert Mandel examines the challenges present in converting military victory into a strategic victory for the state. Mandel states that strategic victory is more than winning on the battlefield but "entails accomplishing the short-term and long-term national, regional, and global goals for which the war was fought."[38] He argues that the six elements of strategic victory are: information control, military deterrence, political self-determination, economic reconstruction, social justice, and diplomatic respect.[39] While he focuses primarily on interstate wars, his model is useful in interventions in civil wars. The two elements most relevant to understanding success in military interventions are military deterrence and social justice. Mandel defines military deterrence as "the extent to which the victor provides military security in the defeated state by deterring any internally or internationally belligerent parties from engaging in violent disruptive behavior due to their anticipation of subsequent punishment by the victor."[40] Equally useful is his definition of social justice as "the extent to which the victor justly manages internal turmoil within the defeated state, particularly volatile ethnic/religious/nationalistic violence, transforming it in the direction of reliance on civil discourse to resolve internal and external disagreements."[41] Thus Mandel provides another way to evaluate interventions, as whether the intervening state was able to achieve his version of strategic victory.

Taylor Seybolt puts a narrower, yet still useful, success criterion forth in his book *Humanitarian Military Intervention: The Conditions for Success and Failure*. He argues that

---

[38]Robert Mandel, *The Meaning of Military Victory* (Boulder, CO: Lynne Rienner Publications, 2006), 16.

[39]Ibid., 17.

[40]Ibid.

[41]Ibid.

15

humanitarian interventions should be evaluated by the amount of lives saved.[42] This also marries up nicely with Regan's two success criteria, of stopping the killing and regional stability.

In *Civil Wars and Foreign Powers: Outside Intervention in Intrastate Conflict*, Patrick Regan develops a model that he argues is able to predict when third party interventions will be successful. Regan's statistical analysis examined 140 intrastate conflicts of which 90 had third parties intervene. The variables he used examine when do third parties tend to intervene, which countries intervene, how often does each country intervene in an conflict, how do they intervene and the number of intervening groups per conflict. Additional variables, such as number of casualties, intensity of the conflict, and number of borders were also analyzed to produce descriptive statistics. Conceptually the variable that closest resembles the topic of this monograph is how states intervene and its effect on the outcome. However, Regan defines the "how" of an intervention as either a military intervention, economic intervention, or a mixed intervention that uses both elements. His work does not examine the structure, organization, or composition of the intervention force quantitatively.

Regan notes that multilateral interventions are different than unilateral and he dedicates an entire chapter to their examination. He states that there are not enough instances of multinational intervention to analyze quantitatively, so instead, he conducts two case studies Zaire in 1967 and El Salvador. He argues that any effort by an intervener to ensure regional stability after the cessation of violent conflict must alter the physical, social, and economic infrastructure, so that it is inclusive and not divisive.[43] To enable this transformation, interventions must be neutral, have the consent of all parties to the conflict, and have a coherently

---

[42]Taylor B. Seybolt, *Humanitarian Military Intervention: The Conditions for Success and Failure* (Oxford: Oxford University Press, 2007).

[43]Regan, 111.

organized and implemented strategy.[44] He then uses his case-studies to test his theory and

concludes that although these variables are not necessary for success their presence increases the

likelihood of it.[45] Of his cases, one was a failure, Zaire and El Salvador was a success. He uses

the cases to test the theory that the variables that affect the probability of success are neutrality

and consent. Following his case-studies he argues that these two variables were crucial to either

the success or failure of intervention. While Civil Wars and Foreign Powers examines both

unilateral and multilateral interventions it does not compare the two to see if one form is more

likely to produce the desired outcome.

Michael W. Doyle and Nicholas Sambanis's *Making War and Building Peace* put forth a

model known as the peacebuilding triangle that they argue may be used to predict when and how

interventions will be successful. The peacebuilding triangle is built around the three main

dimensions of: hostility, local capacities, and international capacity. They then constructed and

coded proxy variables that they used to measure the levels of hostility, local capacity, and

international capacity present in a conflict. This model was then applied to numerous conflicts

and formed the foundation of their case study analysis. While the authors discuss how important

command and control is to effective military and peacekeeping operations, it is not captured in

their statistical analysis.

Doyle and Sambanis do spend significant time discussing how effective command and

control affects the quality of peace operations. They argue that the multilateral nature of UN is

strength with respect to "making, keeping, building, and strategically enforcing a

comprehensively negotiated peace" however is weakness militarily.[46] They agree with and quote

Adam Roberts's assertion that military operations require fast decision making and the ability to

---

[44]Ibid.

[45]Ibid., 131.

[46]Ibid., 189-196.

link operations and intelligence.[47] This is more easily achieved with standing military organizations than any UN apparatus.[48] They then give numerous examples of how the UN is not configured and struggles to wage war as an organization.[49]

Similarly, Adam Lockyear argues that he can predict the affect of an intervention and argues that third party interveners can change the course and nature of a civil war. He states that that civil wars can be understood by analogy and are little different than the duels waged by gladiators in ancient Rome. He argues that the resources provided to a particular fighter determined the tactics employed by each gladiator and affected the result and length of each bout. The actual fighters' size, skill, and background were not influential. He continues, that third party interveners in civil wars similarly tip the balance between competing armed groups in civil war.

However, Lockyear is making a structural argument where resources determine how combatants fight each other. He overly discounts that leaders of the fighting factions are able to choose different strategic approaches to their campaigns. These choices are likely to be affected by relative resources but preferences stemming from cultural, historical, and political beliefs often influence which strategy is chosen. Additionally, he does not offer much evidence to support his argument aside from a single case study.

The RAND Corporation recently completed a study entitled *The UN's Role in Nation-Building* that also contributes to the literature on third party interventions. *The UN's Role in Nation-Building* complements RAND's previous report *America's Role in Nation-Building: From Germany to Iraq* which examines stability operations post World War II focused around seven case studies. A similar approach is applied in *The UN's Role in Nation-Building* in examining UN peace operations while additionally comparing and contrasting UN and US interventions. The

---

[47]Ibid., 189.

[48]Ibid.

[49]Ibid., 196.

authors argue that the UN missions are always undermanned and resourced for what they hope will be a post conflict situation.[50] In contrast, the US approach is usually built on the assumption of the worst case scenario and relies on overwhelming force to establish a secure environment.[51] The UN plans for peacekeeping while the US assumes peace enforcement. They note that the UN has a higher success rate yet their missions have occurred in less demanding circumstances.[52]

As with similar studies, *The UN's Role in Nation-Building* uses a mix of quantitative and qualitative comparisons. They organized their variables as either input or outputs. The inputs they measured were the military presence in peak number of troops, duration of operation, and amounts of civilian police present.[53] The outputs measured were combat related deaths, length of sustained peace, the amount of refugees that returned, democraticization, external assistance, and economic growth.[54] As with other studies organizational structure is not a variable examined in statistical analysis, yet unity of command is mentioned in many of the case studies.

Academics and practitioners alike refer to the quantity of forces used during military operations using a range of terms, to include force ratio, troop density, and boots on the ground density. These terms are largely synonymous and are virtually interchangeable. Force ratio refers to the amount of forces present either relative to the size of the enemy or the population, depending upon the situation and author. Troop density or boots on the ground density, is another way to describe and analyze various intervention forces by their relative size and it usually refers to the amount of land forces relative to the size of the population. This study will examine the works of James T. Quinlivan, Peter J.P. Krause, and John J. McGrath in an attempt to determine a range of thresholds, to enable a comparison of different stability operations relative to each other.

---

[50]Ibid., 29.

[51]Ibid.

[52]Ibid., 30.

[53]Ibid., 21-23.

[54]Ibid., 23-29.

While resources are generally accepted as a key component and a necessary variable, there is still a range of academic and practical opinions about what constitutes the ideal level of manning for stability operations.

Any discussion of troop density should begin with Quinlivan's "Force Requirements in Stability Operations." This article is the source of the stability operations rule of thumb of 20 soldiers per 1000 members of the population. It was widely accepted and still influential today in spite of recent criticism.

Quinlivan begins by arguing that there are no simple answers on force ratios and that ratios should be relative to the population instead of the threat.[55] He argues that his intent is not to prove anything but to illustrate trends by analyzing select cases. From his selected cases he produces three groupings of force ratios of soldiers per 1000 members of the population: 1 to 4, 4 to 10, and greater than 10. Quinlivan's discussion of cases with greater than 10 per 1000 is based on only two episodes consisting of the United Kingdom's interventions in the Malayan Emergency and the troubles in North Ireland, both of which were manning at 20 per 1000. These two paragraphs spawned the widely accepted recommended minimum ratio of 20 per 1000 even though Quinlivan's article does not advocate it. He argues that generating an adequate force ratio is a necessary condition, but in and of itself is not sufficient to achieve stability.[56]

Quinlivan wrote during the mid 1990s post Cold War, when the Balkans and peace operations dominated military discussions. He argued that the increasing size of populations in the third world, combined with rising urbanization would increase the actual amount of troops needed to stabilize an area. If population grows, then the stability force should correspondingly increase. Quinlivan was not arguing to prove what appropriate ratios should be. Instead he was

---

[55]James T. Quinlivan, "Force Requirements in Stability Operations," *Parameters* (Winter 1995): 60.

[56]Ibid.

using ratios to demonstrate that stability is resource intensive with respect to manpower. He then argues that current US Forces levels at the time were barely sufficient to conduct long term stability operations for either a city or country with a population of 1 million people, since it would need one quarter of the available US Army Infantry Battalions. It is somewhat ironic that an article written to argue for expanded force structure became the genesis of the acceptance of 20 per 1000 ratio being widely accepted. Despite being widely accepted by practioners, many of whom do not know the source, academics have criticized Quinlivan's article.

Peter Krause's criticism of Quinlivan focuses on methodology and is useful in many ways. First, he notes that Quinlivan included local security forces inconsistently across cases, causing some ratios to be skewed.[57] Second, the descriptions of the selected cases are "cursory" and thin.[58] Third, Quinlivan does not attempt to resolve the tension between the fact within his selected cases that there were successful stability operations with ratios in the single digits, such as Germany following World War II, yet he seemingly makes an argument that more is better. Finally he questions the selection of these cases and while others were excluded, namely those that exceeded the 20 per 1000 ratio yet failed, such as Algeria.[59] Krause points out that little rigorous scholarship regarding force ratios has occurred as a result of Quinlivan's article and that the research behind it could use "further examination, if not significant revision."[60] John McGrath's *Boots on the Ground* builds on Quinlivan's work with additional research and has similar findings.

---

[57]Peter J. P. Krause, "Troop :Levels in Stability Operations: What We Don't Know," *MIT Center for International Studies* (February 2007): 3.

[58]Ibid.

[59]Ibid.

[60]Ibid.

McGrath argues that the two main factors for determining troop density are the size of the area and population density.[61] Theoretical work on stability operations generally agrees on a ratio of 20 soldiers per 1000 residents as the minimum effective troop density with respect to the size of the population.[62] However, forces levels rarely approach as high a level, as theory recommends. McGrath then compares this theoretical norm to a sample of 10 US stability operations that are all generally regarded as successful operations. His research shows that the average troop density for these operations was 10.76 soldiers per 1000, not the theoretically recommended ration of 20 per 1000. He then proposes an adjusted count of personnel that includes substitute forces in the form of indigenous fighters or police.[63] When local security forces are included, the average troop density ratio shifts to 13.26 soldiers per 1000 of population.[64] For the purposes of this study the historically supported ratio of 13.26 soldiers per 1000 members of the population with be used, the minimum effective manning level. However, the terrain must also be considered when planning troop density.

Policing has its own theory of operations with respect to police density, relative population, and terrain. With respect to population, sampling the largest American municipal police departments produces a ratio of 4.1 officers per 1000 residents.[65] While municipal police are augmented by the state police, the state's police forces are so relatively small that their impact is negligible with respect to police density ratios. For example, California has the largest state

---

[61]John J. McGrath, *Boots on the Ground: Troop Density in Contingency Operations* (Fort Leavenworth, KS: CSI Press, 2006), 2.

[62]Ibid., 1.

[63]Ibid., 101.

[64]Ibid., 103.

[65]Ibid., 83.

police force; yet including them in the ratio calculation only raises the ratio by .20 officers per 1000 residents.[66]

Examining police ratios provide interesting insights when compared to stability operations. Police are manned and require significantly less forces than are required for stability operations.[67] However, if stability operations are conducted where no effective police are present the military will have to assume those duties and planning 4.1 soldiers per 1000 residents is a reasonable low estimate. The 4.1 per 1000 ratio may also be considered as another planning factor, an empirically supportable floor for manning levels during stability operations. However, levels that low would likely require the operational environment to be relatively stable, i.e. peacekeeping not peacemaking.

McGrath demonstrates that many successful contingency operations were manned well below the theoretically recommended ratios.[68] The second half of McGrath's troop density hypothesis is that the area, meaning type and amount of terrain, affect troop density. Through his case study analysis, he concludes that terrain did not affect troop levels and he proceeds to remove it from his list of factors.[69] While terrain may not be useful for explaining the amount of troops in the intervention force, it does appear to affect mission success. Disregarding terrain as a variable is not appropriate when examining coalition stability operations with respect to operational risk. As already discussed the protection afforded to belligerents by being able to hide in rough terrain, foreign sanctuaries, and blend in with the population, does affect the government's and intervention force's ability to suppress insurgency.[70] McGrath only examined

---

[66]Ibid.

[67]Ibid., 84.

[68]McGrath, 91.

[69]Ibid., 97.

[70]James D. Fearon and David D. Laitin, "Ethnicity, Insurgency, and Civil War," *American Political Science Review* 97, no. 1 (February 2003): 79-80.

select, successful operations. Since this monograph includes the force conducting stability operations and the operating environment, rough terrain is appropriate as an independent variable.

Analysis of troop density only examines the quantity of forces while ignoring the role of quality. Not all intervention forces are of equal quality even if countries contribute forces of similar size. One way of differentiating forces qualitatively is to separate interventions conducted by major powers from those that are not. Regan uses this construct in his book *Civil Wars and Foreign Powers*. Using major powers as a variable not only assumes that they have quality militaries but also implies that they have a monopoly with respect to capacity. While it is conceptually useful to recognize the impact of major powers, when comparing results across distinct conflicts other descriptions may lend more clarity and improve analysis. Finding a means to measure military capability would be useful.

Analyzing the above literature on coalition warfare, conflict outcomes, and resources results in the following list of variables for further analysis. The variables for this study are:

1. Intervention can be unilateral, or multinational.

2. Multinational can be an alliance, coalition, or hybrid.

3. Command and Control (C2) structures can be integrated, lead nation, parallel.

4. Mandate must be achievable with given resources and authorities.

5. One way of analyzing resources is to examine force ratios.

6. When directly intervening on the side of the government success is their retaining control and not having ceded territory or sovereignty.

Methodology

This monograph contains a combination of quantitative and qualitative analysis as recommended by Stephen Van Evera in the *Guide to Methods for Students of Political Science* and practiced in the Paul Collier and Nicholas Sambanis's edited volumes, *Understanding Civil War*. Van Evera argues that the three basic methods of testing theories are experimentation, observations using large-*n* analysis, and observation using case study analysis.[71] He notes that experimentation is rarely feasible in political science resulting in a general reliance on two types of observation. It is as unfeasible to conduct experiments during war. However, one could argue that natural experiments are possible within a case if there is change in a key variable, thus enabling a before and after comparison. However, this still poses challenges to validity for it assumes that the operating environment and actors have not changed or adapted during the course of the war. Simply put, the context is not the same during the beginning and end of a conflict. Thus observation is the most appropriate method for this examination.

The two forms of observation have their own attendant strengths and weaknesses when applied to the topic of this monograph. Large-*n* or statistical analysis are often useful analytically when there is sufficiency cases. Van Evera mentions that there should be "several dozen or more".[72] In some instances, there were sufficient cases to instill greater confidence in the results of the quantitative analysis, while others had relatively small sample sizes. However, this only implies the need for case study analysis. Case studies are often used by analysts and appropriate when there are a limited amount of cases to observe.[73] They offer the benefit of examining

---

[71]Stephen Van Evera, *The Guide to Methods for Students of Political Science* (New York: Cornell University Press, 1997), 27.

[72]Ibid., 29.

[73]Ibid.

episodes in detail while still checking to see if events unfolded as predicted by the theory.[74] Van Evera also states that in general, more tests are better than less and that case studies allow the examiner to look for additional commonality across cases to aid in understanding. All of the above informed the decision to use statistical and case study in testing the theory that, multinational operations decrease the likelihood of operational success in stability operations.

The methodology used in this monograph was also influenced by the work of Paul Collier, Anke Hoeffler, and Nicholas Sambanis whose work combines statistical analysis and case studies. In their edited volumes, *Understanding Civil War*, various authors apply the well known Collier-Hoeffler quantitative model of civil war onset to analyze in two ways. The quantitative model results in statistical analysis and is used to select cases systematically for study, while the case studies provide context and aid in explaining the quantitative results. The case studies also provide an opportunity to feedback new or modified variables into their theory and the Collier-Hoeffler model.

The original intention was that the quantitative analysis would aid in generating episodes as good candidates for qualitative examination using case studies. However, the statistical analysis showed that there was not a significant relationship between fighting as a multinational headquarters and campaign success rates. Yet, as the literature review demonstrates, quantitative analysis on this subject had not yet been done and still may be interesting to some.

Each case study follows that same format. They each contain: a brief summary of the context leading up to the intervention, a description of the threat, character of intervention force, the command and control structure, resources, quality of forces, description of fighting and the results of, overall analysis, logic model for the particular intervention, analysis of a particular battle, and conclusion. The monograph then concludes with a comparison of the two cases, an overall summary of the research findings, and suggested areas for further research.

---

[74]Ibid.

Quantitative Analysis

The quantitative analysis centered around two main contingency tables. The first contingency table sought to see if there was a relationship between direct intervention on the side of the government and defeating the insurgency. The second contingency table builds on the first by examining the relationship between whether the intervening force was a coalition or single state aiding the government attempting to defeat the insurgency.

This monograph used the database built by Ben Connable and Martin C. Libicki for the RAND study *How Insurgencies End*.[75] Their research combined a mix of quantitative and qualitative analysis to examine 89 insurgencies. Their work looks at a wide range of variables many of which were similar to the ones used by Fearon and Laitin, i.e. strength of the government and the availability of sanctuary. Their database provides an additional advantage, in that it was recently constructed so it includes current conflicts. The primary reason it was selected is that the data base contained the key variable required for quantitative analysis: the character of the intervener and if the government won.

The RAND data was modified to build the contingency tables used in this monograph. The RAND data set had four possible outcomes: the government won, insurgents won, a mixed settlement, and the conflict was still ongoing.[76] The data set was modified to build the contingency charts in table 1 and table 2. While the outcome of the government won remained unchanged, a new outcome, the government lost, was created by combining the instances where the insurgency won with the mixed settlement outcomes. This was a subjective judgment that anything short of the government defeating the insurgency was a government loss. The survival

---

[75]Ben Connable and Martin C. Libicki, *How Insurgencies End* (Santa Monica, CA: RAND Corporation, 2010).

[76]Ibid., 163.

of the government was not enough to constitute victory, yet surviving and gaining power does constitute, at least a limited victory for the insurgents.

For both contingency tables the three tests used were Chi Squared, Chi Squared with a Yates correction, and the Fisher Exact test. All three tests are appropriate for seeing if the variables on a contingency chart are related, however standard Chi Squared tests are not recommend for data sets with relatively small sample sizes. The Chi Squared test with Yates correction and Fisher's Exact test are generally considered more appropriate and preferred for examining smaller samples. The Fisher Exact test is generally used for samples smaller than 30, thus it is the most appropriate for table 2.

The research questions results in a hypothesis, that intervening on the side of the government is associated with the government defeating the insurgency. The corresponding null hypothesis is:

H0: Interventions on the side of the government in counterinsurgencies are not related to the government losing.

As shown on table 1, all three tests produce results that are not statistically significant, thus failing to reject the null hypothesis. Simply put, the statistics show that there is no relation between intervening on the side of the government and defeating the insurgency.

Table 1.   Contingency Table Comparing the War's Outcome
            with Outside Intervention

	Direct Intervener	No Direct Intervention	Total
Government Wins	4	24	28
Government Loses	17	44	61
Total	21	68	89

Fisher Exact Test 2 tailed	.1894		
Chi Squared w/Yates correction	1.283	two-tailed P value	0.2574
Chi Squared	1.964	two-tailed P value	0.1611

Source: Created by Author.

The next step was to analyze whether there was an association between intervening on the side of the government as a multinational force and defeating the insurgency. The hypothesis was that a multinational force was more likely to be defeated by the insurgency. The corresponding null hypothesis is:

H0: Multinational interventions on the side of the government in counterinsurgencies are not related to the government losing.

As shown in table 2, all three tests produce results that are not statistically significant, thus failing to reject the null hypothesis. Simply put, the statistics show that there is no relation between the structure of the intervention force, either unilateral or multinational, and successfully defeating an insurgency.

Table 2. Contingency Table Comparing the Operational Effectiveness
of Resources, Command and Control

	Single Intervener	Multi-National Intervener	Total
Government Wins	4	1	5
Government Loses	15	4	19
Total	19	5	24

Fisher Exact Test 2 tailed	1.000		
Chi Squared w/Yates correction	0.003	two-tailed P value	0.9589
Chi Squared	0.003	two-tailed P value	0.9589

Source: Created by Author

So how do we account for this? Unity of command is a long standing, historically accepted principle of war that causes us to assume that all things being equal, a unilateral force should have an advantage and greater likelihood of success when compared to a multinational intervention force. So why does the quantitative analysis reflect an advantage for the more unified command?

A cursory examination of the conflicts represented in the data set shows that the similarities and commonalities across these wars are extremely limited. The one instance in the data set where a multinational force intervened on the side of the government and the government won was the Congolese Civil War of 1960-1964. Within the RAND data set the Congolese Civil War is listed as Congo/Katanga. The conflicts where a multinational force intervened on the side of the government and the government lost, or had a mixed settlement, are: Laos (1960-1975), Liberia (1989-1997), Bosnia (1992-1995), and the Congo anti-Kabila (1998-2003). These are very distinct and different conflicts.

Case Study Selection

While all five instances of a multinational intervention on the side of the government are suitable candidates for further examination, the limited scope of this monograph led to winnowing it down to cases: the Congolese Civil War of 1960-1965 and the civil war in Bosnia Herzegovina. These were selected for two main reasons. The first being that they were both UN led multinational forces. The second is they represent the two possible outcomes, either a government win or a loss, in the Congo the government defeated the Katangan secession whereas the United Nations Protection Force (UNPROFOR) was not victorious. However, the outcomes of these wars are debatable making them good candidates for case studies. To illustrate this point we can compare the RAND's *How Insurgencies End* database coding to some other well known authors. The Congolese Civil War of 1960-1965 was coded as a government win in RAND's *How Insurgencies End* but Michael W. Doyle and Nicholas Sambanis categorize it largely a peacemaking failure in their book *Making War and Building Peace*. So who is right? In many ways, they both are. These episodes illustrate not only the difficulties in defining victory in stability operations but also how challenging it is to design and resource a successful intervention.

The Congo Crisis 1960-1965

"The Republic of the Congo failed almost from the moment of its birth. Within days of the Congo's independence its army mutinied, the remaining white administrators fled, the administration and the economy collapsed, Belgian paratroops invaded, and the mineral-rich province of Katanga seceded."[77]

The above aptly summarizes how the Congo failed only 14 days after gaining its independence resulting in a request for UN assistance. On July 14, 1960 the United Nations Security Council (UNSC) adopted Resolution 143 authorizing the Secretary-General to organize military and technical assistance to the Congolese Government while calling on Belgium to withdraw its troops.[78] What follows is a brief description of the situation in the Congo prior to its independence and UN intervention, some of the variables presented, analysis of the threat, the character of the intervention force, the command and control structure, the quality of United Nations Operations in the Congo (ONUC) forces, overall analysis, and conclusion.

The Belgian colonial legacy resulted in a general lack of development across the board that left the Congo unprepared for independence. "The Republic of the Congo became a state before it became a nation."[79] The Free State of the Congo was colonized by Belgian King Leopold II as his personal possession in 1885 and was later transferred to the Belgian Government for administration in 1907.[80] However, since colonization was motivated by resource extraction, the economy, followed by primary education were the only sectors that received

---

[77]James Dobbins, Seth G. Jones, Keith Crane, Andrew Rathmell, Brett Steele, Richard Teltschik, and Anga Timilsina, *The UN's Role in Nation-Building: From the Congo to Iraq* (Santa Monica, CA: RAND Corporation, 2005), xv.

[78]Ernest W. Lefever, *Crisis in the Congo: A United Nations Force in Action* (Washington, DC: Brookings Institute, 1965), 11.

[79]Lefever, 5.

[80]Department of State, Bureau of African Affairs, "Background Note: The Democratic Republic of the Congo," http://www.state.gov/r/pa/ei/bgn/2823.htm (accessed July 26, 2012).

significant development. Lack of development of the local security forces would prove to have devastating effects.

Belgium originally planned a long transition to the Congo from colonial rule to independence as they began examining the issue in the late 1950s. However, the Belgian government and colony were both impacted by other independence movements elsewhere in Africa. The Congolese independence movement grew and January 1959 saw the first serious anti-government riots in Leopoldville. In January 1960, a four year transition to independence plan put forth by Belgium was rejected by the Congolese. In the face of rising pressure Belgium conceded to the Congolese requests for immediate independence and set June 30, 1960 as the transition date. This has been described as a recipe for disaster where the colonial administration was unprepared to deal with the fervor of the independence movement, while conversely those seeking independence found themselves completely unprepared for the for responsibilities of governing.[81]

The crisis in the Congo arguably started three days after independence on July 2, 1960 when tribal riots erupted in the capital Leopoldville and Luluabourg. This was followed by a mutiny of the Congolese soldiers in the Armeé National Congolaise (ANC) against their Belgian officers, which was probably encouraged by the communist bloc agents.[82] Belgian officials tried, to no avail, to convince the new government and Prime Minister Lumumba to allow the Belgian troops garrisoned at their remaining two bases to help restore order and protect the panicked Belgian civilians and their property. A frustrated Belgium reinforced its garrisons with two additional two and half companies of paratroopers on July 9, against with the approval of the

---

[81]Jane Boulden, *Peace Enforcement: The United Nations Experience in Congo, Somalia, and Bosnia* (Westport, CT: Praeger Publishers, 2001), 22.

[82]Lefever, 11.

Congolese government after five days of diplomacy failed to garner permission.[83] While the deployment did not necessarily violate the Treaty of Friendship between the two countries, the Belgian military operations outside their bases, in an attempt to restore order and protect Belgian lives was and would prove to be controversial locally and abroad.[84]

Making matters worse, on July 11 the Provincial President Moise Tshombe declared that Katanga was independent of the Congo. Tshombe claimed to be breaking away from the chaos that was consuming the Congo, accused Lumumba of colluding with the Communists, criticized the US for not supporting Katanga, and requested Belgian military aid.[85] Tshombe did not consult the population and they were not unified in their desire for independence. Katanga was simultaneously crucial and a challenge. It was a vital state economically, largely due to its mineral wealth and attendant foreign investment. Katanga produced eight percent of the world's copper, 60 percent of its cobalt, and various other minerals.

In the face of the mounting chaos and on the advice of the American Ambassador-designate Clare H. Timberlake, Lumumba makes a verbal request for UN assistance to Dr. Ralph Bunche, UN Undersecretary for Special Political Affairs, who was presently representing the Secretary-General in the Congo. The next day an official cable sent to the Secretary-General signed by both President Joseph Kasavubu and Prime Minister Patrice Lumumba requesting "urgent U.N. military assistance because of Belgian aggression and Belgian support of Katangan secession."[86] This resulted in United Nations Security Council Resolution (UNSCR) S/4387

---

[83]Lefever, 11.

[84]Ibid.

[85]Ibid., 12.

[86]Ibid., 13.

authorizing the Secretary-General to organize military assistance and technical aid, thus launching the UN into its largest and most complex operation to date.[87]

Unfortunately, ONUC was deploying into a political situation that was rapidly deteriorating and would continue to do so for nearly a year. Lumumba was a cantankerous personality and was the center of the political storm.[88] He openly clashed with Hammarskjöld and criticized the UN for not being active enough while he sought and gained military aid from the Soviet Union.[89] Lumumba also clashed with President Kasavubu, who leaned towards the West for support and eventually dismissed Lumumba as the Prime Minister.[90] The political turmoil caused an 11 month constitutional crisis, with no clear central government during which time the country fractured into four competing sectors. Two sectors, Leopoldville and Stanleyville, were led by Kasavubu and Lumumba respectively with each claiming to be the rightful leader of the Congo.[91] The other two regions, Katanga and South Kasai, were secessionist and led by Moise Tschombe and Albert Kaloniji.

Eventually the constitutional crisis was resolved, when the Assembly and Senate of the Congo unanimously approved Kasavubu's appointment of Cyrille Adoula as the Prime Minister on August 2, 1961.[92] With power somewhat consolidated, the Congolese Government shifted its attention to the Katanga issue and pressured the UN mission to act in kind. However, there was still disagreement between what needed to happen first. The Secretary-General's first priority was

---

[87]Ibid., 15.

[88]Gordon, J. King, *The United Nations in the Congo: A Quest for Peace* (Washington, DC: Carnegie Endowment for International Peace, 1962), 52-55.

[89]Ibid.

[90]Ibid.

[91]Lefever, 48-51. The leadership in Leopoldville and Stanleyville was tumultuous and morphed over time. The new chief of staff of the Army Joseph Mobutu formed a loose coalition with President Kasavubu in Leopoldville. When the Stanleyville leader, Patrice Lumumba, was murdered under suspicious circumstances he was replaced by his lieutenant Antoine Gizenga.

[92]Lefever, 54.

expelling foreign military personnel not connected with the UN mission but the Adoula Government was focused on ending Katanga's secession.[93] Offensive operations began despite disagreement about which problem should be the priority. This began a new phase of the operation, marked by offensive operations and increased activity of ONUC. The four offensive operations were Rumpunch, Morthor, Unokat, and Grand Slam with each producing varying results.

Description of the threat

ONUC had to contend with various armed groups as it attempted to implement its mandate. Those groups included the Belgian forces, foreign mercenaries, separatists, and those vying for control of the government. When civil war broke out following independence, Belgium used the forces still garrisoned in the Congo in an attempt to protect the Belgians still living in the Congo, Belgian business interests, and private property. The ANC, mutinied against its completely Belgian Officer Corps. This mutiny resulted in the breakdown of discipline within the ANC and the ability of the central government to control them. Over time the ANC would turn against the ONUC due to ONUC's failure to end the Katangan secession.[94] Internal to the Congo, ONUC had to contend with an aggressive local army, secessionists, and ethnic violence along tribal lines in certain areas.

The mercenary problem in the Congo had multiple facets yet largely centered around the Katanga region. The Congo had become a civil war with various factions vying for control of the state, i.e. forces under Lumumba, while others attempted to secede to include Katanga and South Kasai. Some mercenaries were Belgian military forces who had been seconded to Katanga or had removed their Belgian uniforms and continued to fight. Other mercenaries included fighters from

---

[93]Ibid., 72-73.
[94]Boulden, 33.

Europe, who were usually French, which were referred to as *paras* or ultras. These European mercenaries were hardcore believers who were upset about the French loss in Algeria and were continuing the fight in other parts of colonized Africa. While the mandate primarily recognized two types of belligerents, secessionists and Belgian mercenaries, the reality was more complex and contained various armed actors fighting for different reasons.

Character of the Intervention Force

Analyzing resources available presents a challenge, in that troops available, external support, and contributing nations often changed during the four year operation. However, this is not uncommon during multinational operations of any length. While the size and composition often changed, the force generally ranging from 15,000 to nearly 20,000.[95] During ONUC, the Congo's population was 17 million. When their population of 17 million is divided by a peak of ONUC forces of nearly 20,000, results in a ratio of one soldier per 850 people in the population. This converts to troop density of 1.18 per 1000 members of the population. This force ratio is well below all of the various ratios recommended in the literature review. In general, the ONUC was a light infantry force. Air movement was provided by means of charter plans or was at times contributed on a case by case basis. While the UN did have limited internal air movement capability, it initially did not have any air attack or fighter assets.

For all of its shortcomings, the speed in which ONUC was formed and deployed is still amazing more than 50 years later. Merely one day after the resolution was approved 770 Ghanaians and 593 Tunisians were deployed to the Congo with airlift provided by the British and US Air Force respectively.[96] In a month's time, the force grew to more than 14,000 troops from

---

[95]Indar Jit Rikhye, *Military Advisor to the Secretary-General* (New York: St. Martin's Press, 1993), 331.

[96]Lefever, 31.

24 states.[97] And while the US did not contribute troops, the US Air Force transported 9,213 members of ONUC in the first month, in what was at the time the single greatest airlift executed by a country.[98]

C2 Structure

At first glance the command and control structure of ONUC seems simple and efficient. At the top of the hierarchy was the UNSC, who authorized the UN military mission and with the Secretary-General Hag Hammarskjold overseeing the UN mission. Hammarskjold interpreted the mandate as the UN Force being subordinate to the Security Council and not the host nation. Working under Hammarskjold as the lead for the UN mission in the Congo was his Special Representative, a position which was later renamed the Officer-In-Charge. The Officer-In-Charge directed all three subordinate, the UN Chief of Civilian Operations, the Commander of the United Nations Force (UNF), and the Chief Administrative Officer. The Commander of the UNF commandeered the subordinate military contingents below him and was responsible for coordination with the UN civilian operations and administration sections (see figure 1). However, examining the history of the ONUC mission highlights that the command and control structure is less clear and efficient than its organization chart implies.

Leadership across various levels was fairly turbulent with frequent changes. The Secretary-General proved to be a relatively constituent and unifying force across the operation. However, even the Secretary-General changed following Hammarskjold's death in an airplane accident enroute to negotiate a possible cease fire with Tshombe and was succeeded by U Thant. In less than four years, nine different people led the operation in the Congo as the UN Officer in

---

[97]Ibid.

[98]Ibid.

Charge.[99] Additionally five different people lead the military mission as the UN Force Commander, with the Katanga Operation having four commanders over time. It is hard to imagine that this amount of turnover amongst the senior leaders of the policy and military efforts did not negatively affect the UN operations.

Figure 1.   ONUC Chain of Command

Source: Created by author, data from Indar Jit Rikhye, *Military Advisor to the Secretary-General* (New York: St. Martin's Press, 1993); Trevor Findlay, *The Blue Helmets' First War? Use of Force by the UN in the Congo 1960-1964* (Clementsport: Canadian Peacekeeping Press, 1999), 8.

Mandate

The UN Security Resolutions relative to the Congo were few in number and overall established a mandate that was sufficiently broad (vauge) enough that the UNSC would approve it, yet provided sufficient authority to the Secretary-General and ONUC to respond to the crisis.

---

[99]Lefever, 200-01.

Over time, the mandate became less vague, was more specific in its direction, and authorized and directed the use of force.

The core of the initial mandate contained in Resolution 143 called on Belgium to withdraw its troops from the Congo and for the Secretary-General to take the necessary steps, in consultation with the Government of the Congo, to provide them with the necessary military assistance.[100] The next Resolution 145, did not change the nature of the mandate for ONUC, and served mostly to reaffirm the previous resolution, further urged a hasty Belgian withdrawal, tasked the Secretary-General to take "all necessary action" to ensure the Belgians did leave, and called up the member states to refrain from interfering in the Congo's internal matters.[101] Resolution 146 was explicit that the UN was to enter Katanga, however was not to be a party to or intervene in or attempt to influence the outcome of the internal conflict.[102] While these early resolutions did not explicitly authorize the use of force, the next round of resolutions did, reflecting how the situation in the Congo had changed, namely the repeated harassment of UN troops.

Resolution 161 explicitly authorized the use of force and provided the most significant change to the ONUC mandate.[103] The military advisor to the Secretary-General, General Indar Jit Rikhye, observed that this change produced two options for the use of force. The first was that ONUC could continue operating in the same manner, using force in self-defense. The other option would be to use force as part of military initiative.[104]

---

[100]Boulden, 23-24; United Nations. Security Council, Resolution 143.

[101]Boulden, 25; United Nations, Security Council Resolution 145 (S/4405), *The Congo Question*, July 22, 1960, 879th meeting.

[102]Boulden, 26; United Nations, Security Council. Resolution 156 (S/4491), *Question Related to the Dominique Republic*, September 9, 1960, 895th meeting.

[103]United Nations, Security Council. Resolution 161 (S/4741), *The Congo Question*, February 21, 1961.

[104]Boulden, 32.

Overall the mandate did not hinder ONUC, but the Secretary-General's interpretation and self imposed rules of engagement did. Findlay argues that when ONUC began using force offensively, that they transitioned from a peacekeeping to peace enforcement.[105]

Description of Fighting and the Results

In Katanga, the ONUC conducted four main offensives known as Operations Rumpunch, Mothor, Unokat, and Grand Slam. Operations Rumpunch and Mothor focused on capturing mercenaries whereas Unokat and Grand Slam were offenses directed against the secessionist's genderarmie forces. To return the secessionist Katanga province back to government control. The ONUC's "Operation Grand Slam" was an attack into Katanga that effectively reunited the breakaway province back into the Congo.[106]

The first of these missions, Operation Rumpunch, began on August 28, 1961 and its purpose was to apprehend and evacuate Belgian forces from Katanga. The mission to apprehend was not truly offensive, in that the UN forces did not plan to use force and were still generally committed to only using force in self-defense. Rumpunch up surprised the Belgian forces, which resulted in between 70 to 100 Belgians being apprehended without any shooting.[107] However, momentum was lost when deals where brokered with the Belgian consul and Tshombe with the UN representative in Katanga, Conor Cruise O'Brien, halting the operation. While Tshombe kept his promise to publicly encourage cooperation, behind the scenes they continued "pacification" killings. The Belgian government also failed to uphold its promise to withdraw, claiming that they could not force Belgian "nationals" to leave.

---

[105]Trevor Findlay, *The Blue Helmets' First War? Use of Force by the UN in the Congo 1960-1964* (Clementsport: Canadian Peacekeeping Press, 1999), 109.

[106]Michael W. Doyle, and Nicholas Sambanis, *Making War and Building Peace* (Princeton, NJ: Princeton University Press, 2006), 179.

[107]Findlay, *The Blue Helmets' First War*, 97-97.

There is no disagreement that the ONUC forces lost Round One, Operation Mothor, and that the mission overall was an unmitigated disaster militarily and politically. However, there is still much confusion and controversy surrounding who authorized Mothor, who knew about it, and what the true objectives of the operation were.[108] Yet there is general agreement on what occurred during the fighting.

Operation Mothor's undisputed military objectives included seizing the radio station, Post Office, and Sûreté, detaining foreign fighters and some key political leaders. The political objectives are still subject to debate with one side arguing that the goal was removing foreign fighters, whereas the other contests that the real aim was to end the Katangan secession. Even the tactics were controversial within the ONUC forces, some of whom objected that offensive nature conflicted with their peacekeeping mandate, while others complained about being constrained to only use force in self-defense during an offense, while attempting to seize objectives held by armed Katangans.[109] The ONUC forces were handed a flawed concept of operations of doing a larger version of Rumpunch, knowingly backing into the need to use force, combined with seizing the key terrain of the radio station, and some political leaders will end the secession and meet little resistance. Unfortunately for the ONUC forces, their political leaders assumptions proved false and they found themselves in an eight day long battle in which they were overmatched.

Mothor began at 4 a.m. on September 13, 1961. Early on ONUC was successful in achieving some of its objectives in that it was able to seize the radio station, post office, and Sûreté, though not without cost. Indian troops came under attack while trying to negotiate with Katangan paratroopers at the post office, and panicked when a sniper killed one of their men.[110]

---

[108]Ibid., 99.

[109]Ibid., 99-101.

[110]Ibid., 102.

This sparked a fire fight in which the Indians overreacted, shot at an ambulance, and allegedly murdered some of the captured secessionists.[111] Also, Katangan forces led by white officers were able to surround and isolate a company of 150 Irish soldiers and what would develop into the Battle of Jadotville. This battle ran from September 13 to 17 and ended after multiple ONUC relief convoys were repelled forcing the Irish to surrender when they ran out of water and ammunition. The last significant military embarrassment was the fact that ONUC forces, UN personnel and facilities suffered repeated harassing attacks for eight days from a single Katangan jet with a Belgian pilot. The UN had no fighter jets or air defense assets to counter the air attacks. When Ethiopia agreed to provide air support, the UN was unable to secure over flight rights through Uganda due to British objections.[112] When Hammarskjöld arrived, his orders to stop the offense where unable to stop the fighting, as ONUC had to repeatedly use force in self-defense as they continued to be attacked.

Mothor was also a political embarrassment within the theater of operation and internationally. With respect to operations in theater, it is fairly apparent, as Finley argues, that the UN Headquarters in New York had lost control of the situation in the Congo.[113] Numerous accounts argue that the offense was initiated by local UN leaders either in coordination with the central government or in response to threats from the central government, to attack into Katanga if the UN did not. O'Brien has continually maintained the Hammarskjöld not only knew about the offense but also directed it, only to back away from it when it met stiff Katangan resistance. While possible, this seems unlikely and wholly inconsistent with Hammarskjöld's emphasis on neutrality and reluctance to use force.

---

[111]Ibid.

[112]Ibid., 106.

[113] Ibid, 103.

Operation Mothor produced two final negative outcomes for the UN. Determined to end the fighting Hammarskjöld flew to meet with Tshombe to attempt to negotiate a ceasefire. Hammarskjöld's plane crashed killing him and all others on board. Following Hammarskjöld's tragic death, the negotiations continued with replacement officials who were under duress and bargaining from a position of weakness. While Tshombe did agree to a ceasefire, the conditions of which furthered the image that ONUC had lost to his Katangan forces, largely halted ONUC military activity in Katanga, and it bought Tshombe additional time to consolidate his power.

After Mothor and in the face of increased attacks and aggression against UN forces, ONUC became more active militarily due to a stronger mandate and a new Secretary-General. Gendarme increased its attacks against ONUC to include "sniper attacks, aerial attacks, and ground assaults, and the detention of a number of UN personnel."[114] In November 1961, The UNSC issued Resolution 169 that reaffirmed the previous resolutions, clarified objectives, and expanded the authorized use of force. This was a dramatic shift. The UNSC was no longer trying to appear neutral and had chosen to side with the central government and might use force to deal with the Katanga secession. U Thant became the UN Secretary-General following the tragic death of Hammarskjöld in the plane crash and brought with him a different interpretation of the UN mission and mandate. U Thant was less concerned with remaining impartial and more willing to use force. This combination of a modified mandate and new leadership enabled what would be the two most aggressive ONUC missions in the Congo; Operations Unokat and Grand Slam.

Unokat Round Two

Round two, Operation Unokat was conducted on December 5 to 18, 1961. Secretary-General U Thant's instructions were "to take necessary action to ensure the freedom of movement of the UN troops and to restore law and order in Katanga so that the UN resolutions could be

---

[114]Boulden, 37.

implemented." [115]Unokat began as a defensive operation to hold their current positions while awaiting reinforcements from December 5 to 15.[116] Round Two began with an Indian unit removing the roadblock between the airport and the UN Headquarters, to which the Katangan forces responded with attacks against UNF positions using heavy mortars, machines guns, and rifles.[117] Clashes of various size, intensity, and methods, including both ground and air, would continue on both sides; however the ONUC ground forces were primarily on the defensive, focused on defending their positions while awaiting reinforcements.[118]

ONUC began what would be a three day offensive operation with the arrival of reinforcements at the Elisabethville garrison on December 17, 1961. The ONUC offensive was successful and UNF proved to be superior to the Katangan forces. Key events and objectives were the clearing of a zone on both sides of the road which connected the headquarters and the airport by an Indian Gurkha Unit, the main Katanga base at Camp Massart was seized by Swedish forces, the tunnel under the railroad was taken by Irish troops, and the Lido area and road to the border with Rhodesia were taken by Ethiopian forces.[119] Just prior to Thant's ordering a ceasefire to allow for the resumption of negotiations between Tshombe and Adoula, UN forces had begun patrolling the streets of Elisabethville with armored vehicles to reestablish order.[120] Unokat was qualitatively different from Mothor, being that it was offensive in nature, involved significantly more troops, planes for airstrikes, and the on scene commander, Brigadier Raja was permitted greater latitude allowing his forces to seize the initiative.[121]

---

[115]Ibid.

[116]Ibid.

[117]Lefever, 94.

[118]Ibid., 94-96.

[119]Ibid., 96-97.

[120]Ibid., 96-97.

[121]Ibid., 97.

A year of relative peace occurred during the interlude between Round Two and Round Three with the ONUC under U Thant's leadership assisting the central government in maintaining law in order throughout most of the Congo.[122] Stanleville was again brought under control and a tenuous ceasefire held while Tshombe and the Adoula Government continued negotiations.[123] However, Tshombe was merely using the ceasefire to stall while he grew his forces.[124] Eventually Tshombe's harassing attacks would steadily increase over time until they were no longer acceptable.

Round Three, Operation Grand Slam, began on December 28, 1962 as response to Katangan gendarme attacks on UN observation posts in Elisabethville, on December 24, 1962. Grand Slam was similar to Unokat in that its first phase was focused on re-establishing freedom of movement by removing roadblocks and Katangan attack positions. The second phase focused on expanding UN control in Katanga to include the cities of Kipushi and Jadotville.[125]

ONUC forces were able to expand their control with surprising ease throughout the province. However, the relative speed of movement produced a political flair up when ONUC forces, seeking to maintain the initiative pressed across the Lufira River and entered Jadotville. The UNF column had been ordered by the UN Headquarters in New York to halt on the near side of the river. When the Commander, Brigadier Noronha received the instructions his unit was in contact with Katanga forces and taking fire while it straddled the river. Assessing the situation he ordered the rest of his forces to cross and meeting little resistance they seized Jadotville to cheering crowds. Following an investigation by the Undersecretary for Special Political Affairs, Ralph Bunche, that concluded the incident was not a case of insubordination but rather a

---

[122]Findlay, *The Blue Helmets' First War*, 123-131.

[123]Ibid., 123.

[124]Ibid., 124.

[125]Boulden, 39.

symptom of an organizational failing to communicate.[126] U Thant in a later report acknowledge that is was a sound military decision in seizing and maintaining the initiative and that it added to the remarkable success and low cost of the operation.[127]

Throughout early January, UNF continued in their efforts to expand their freedom of movement and secure major towns. These successes prompted varying reactions from Tshombe who at times seemed willing to concede defeat and conversely threatened a scorched earth campaign. On January 17, 1963, Tshombe met with ONUC officials and agreed to their entry into his last major holding, the town of Kolwezi and to the surrender of the gendarmerie weapons.[128] The insurrection effectively ended with the end of Grand Slam, when UN forces entered Kolwezi on January 21, 1963.[129]

Broad Analysis

The Congo appears to provide another example where multinational forces were able to successfully mount an offense against standing forces but struggled to eliminate all of the rebellion. While ONUC was successful in helping to protect what it recognized as the government of the Congo and maintaining its territorial integrity, it did not resolve the conflict or build a lasting peace. Doyle and Sambanis argue that UNOC left before the real work of peacekeeping had began and as a result of this "peace*building* failure, several episodes of large-scale violence, including civil war, took place in the 1960s and 1970s, after which Mobutu was able to secure his autocracy."[130]

---

[126]Boulden, 40.

[127]Lefever, 111-112.

[128]Ibid., 110.

[129]Lefever 110-111; Boulden 40.

[130]Doyle and Sambanis, 183.

47

There were repeated command and control issues that reduced operational effectiveness between the Secretary-General and ONUC and between ONUC and the UNF and its subordinate contingents.[131] The Secretary-General lost strategic control of ONUC three times.[132] Despite having a UNF Headquarters, the national contingents were not unified in any meaningful way. UNF Headquarters appears to have had no real control during operations, aside from ordering them to start and assigning the objectives. One of the UNF Commanders, Major General Carl Carlsson von Horn described his force as "an armed mob in which logic, military principles–even common sense–took second place to political favours."[133] This lack of control and synchronization made UNF a very blunt, inefficient tool.

The UN intervention in the Congo can be viewed as a failure if we apply Regan's pragmatic definition that success, achieving the broad political goals of stopping the fighting and regional stability, due the continued and repeated presence of fighting in and around the Congo. Doyle and Sambanis argue, that can be considered a success only in the "narrow sense of achieving its goal of holding the country together" but point out that recurring violent rebellions and Mobutu's later violent repression of political dissent, are indicative of a failure to build peace.[134] Yet the continued violence is likely the result of combination of factors that can be attributed to the rapid decolonization that left the Congo largely without the ability to effectively govern, administer, and provide internal security. These issues were well beyond the mandate and resources of the ONUC. No one was nation building.

---

[131]Findlay, *The Blue Helmets' First War*, 152.

[132]Ibid.

[133]Scott Taylor, and Brian Nolan, *Tested Mettle: Canada's Peacekeepers at War* (Ottawa, Canada: Esprit De Corps Books, 1998), 16.

[134]Doyle and Sambanis, 183.

Battle Analysis: Mothor

Operation Mothor illustrates issues within ONUC stemming from a lack of resources, lack of will, and lack of unity of command. With respect to resources ONUC suffered during Mothor due to a lack of air power or air defense assets, to counter the one Katangan plane that attacked them with impunity. Additionally, the failed attempts to rescue the surrounded Irish Company highlights how the lightly armed ONUC had limited combat power. The limited amount of resources reduced Mothor's odds of success before it even began.

Mothor also suffered from a lack of will to use force. It appears that ONUC leadership ordered an offensive, but told their forces not to attack or fire. The neutralist interpretation of the mandate and rules of engagement cause ONUC leaders to place forces in situations where they hoped the belligerents would engage them, so that ONUC could return fire. Understandably, some of the forces were not thrilled about a mission whose apparent goal was to get them attacked. Prior to the mission an Indian Battalion Commander asked a superior "Must my unit be cut down just to demonstrate that the UN is peaceful?"[135]

Unity of command was not present during Mothor and increased confusion. It is still not clear who really ordered Operation Mothor. However, it is apparent that very little planning occurred, with the plan resembling just simply doing more they did in Rumpunch. Sadly, the lack of will to use force and issues with command and control could have been resolved internal to ONUC as they were under U Thant's leadership.

Conclusion

ONUC was successful in that they eventually were able to help stop the killing and improved regional stability. The Katangan secession was defeated largely to ONUC's efforts. However, this success was aided by two crucial factors. The first was that fight between the

---

[135]Findlay, *The Blue Helmets' First War*, 101.

49

government forces, augmented by ONUC, against Katanga was conventional in nature. These were not insurgents hiding amongst the population striking from the shadows, but were organized and fought more as standing army, albeit an irregular one. The second crucial factor was that the Katanga fighters had a relative low will to fight. This is evident in their actions. At levels they chose to give up fighting instead of regenerating their lost forces and continuing to fight. Che Guevara also made similar criticisms and judgments, that the Katangans had no real will to fight.[136]

At the operational level, ONUC struggled do to their own organizational lack of will. There long held desire to remain neutral and lack of will to use force greatly limited their effectiveness early. This stands in stark contrast when compared to operations under U Thant's leadership, such as Grand Slam where ONUC proved capable of defeating their adversaries when allowed to. The negative effects of this lack of will were magnified by the turbulent, command and control. The ad hoc command and control combined with frequent changing of UN political leadership in country, increased the challenge for ONUC of successfully using its military resources.

ONUC's overall effectiveness was routinely limited by a general lack of resources. They did not have enough manpower to police the entire countryside nor protect much of the population when rule of law broke down. Members of ONUC were at times taken hostage, beaten or murdered by belligerents with local superiority. Additionally the lack of air power and heavy weapons also limited ONUC and resulted in numerous tactical setbacks such as at Jadotville.

ONUC has been criticized for failing to address the root causes of conflict in the Congo and aiding in setting the conditions for violence in the Congo and regionally. While there is something to these criticisms it seems unlikely that any military intervention could have solved

---

[136]Ernesto "Che" Guevara, *The African Dream: The Diaries of the Revolutionary War in the Congo* (New York: Grove Press, 2000).

the severe internal issues in the Congo. The Congo was so severely underdeveloped politically, economically, and socially that it seemed a peacefully transition to a functioning state with good governance seems impossible. Blank was correct in his assessment that the Congo became a state before it became a nation. Unfortunately this would produce long term conditions that enabled repression and violence.

Bosnia Case Study UNPROFOR

Overview Road to War, prior to Intervention

While conflict and tension has a long, significant history in the Balkans, the following

analysis begins with Slovenia and Croatia declaring their independence from the former

Yugoslavia and ends with the Dayton Accords and transition to the Implementation Force. The

dissolution of Yugoslavia resulted in multiple groups competing for varying degrees of

sovereignty with those groups being Serbs, Croatians, and Bosnian Muslims. Serbia was the

largest remaining republic and controlled the Yugoslav People's Army (JNA) that they used to try

to prevent the other republics from seceding.[137] The JNA assisted Croatian Serbs in fierce

fighting against the newly established Croatian Government until signing a cease-fire agreement

in November 1991.[138] The Secretary-General advocated for quickly dispatching a peacekeeping

force stressing that the risk of failure, due to lack of cooperation, was less grievous than the

danger of waiting to intervene posed to the tenuous cease-fire agreement.[139] The UNSC approved

his report and established UNPROFOR six days later, on February 21, 1992 with resolution

743.[140] The initial resolution mandated that UNPROFOR help:

> (1) supervise the withdrawal of the JNA and demilitarize the areas in Croatia occupied by
> Croatian Serbs, (2) return the displaced who fled from their homes in these areas, and (3)
> monitor human rights in these areas. UNPROFOR in Croatia was authorized primarily
> under Chapter VI of the UN Charter, which allows only peaceful means to carry out
> mandates.[141]

---

[137]Government Accountability Office, GAO/NSIAD-95-148BR, *Update on the Situation in the Former Yugoslavia* (Washington, DC: General Accounting Office, May 1995), 1.

[138]Ibid.

[139]United Nations, Department of Public Information, *Former Yugoslav-UNPROFOR*, September 1996, http://www.un.org/Depts/DPKO/Missions/unprof_b.htm (accessed November 17, 2012), 2.

[140]Ibid.

[141]Government Accountability Office, 1.

Politics continued to influence the amount of fighting in the former Yugoslavia. Whereas the international recognition of Croatia helped end the war there, the Bosnian referendum choosing independence, sparked an attack by Bosnian Serbs.[142]

Description of the Threat

UNPROFOR often found itself facing multiple adversaries, to include some of the very people they were trying to protect. Serb fighters came in three main varieties: Serb Military, Serb Paramilitary, and ethnic Serbs who joined as irregulars. Bosnian Muslim combatants were either Bosnian Military or local militia. Croatian combatants were primarily local militia, that was at times reinforced by regular units from Croatia. UNPROFOR was hard pressed to find allies amongst these groups. For example, when Serb attacks caused Dutch forces to withdraw from their outposts in Srebrenica, the Dutch were then attacked by Bosnian militia who did not want them to abandon their positions.[143]

Amongst the three warring parties, the Serbs were clearly the most prepared, organized, and equipped for battle. Serbian strategy used a combination of regular forces, paramilitary forces, and armed elements of the population. Following the formation of the new federal state of Yugoslavia, that contained only Serbia and Montenegro, Slobodan Milosevic maintained control of the JNA due to its being primarily comprised of ethnic Serbs. The Serb Republic was formed in Bosnia as a reaction to the Bosnian independence referendum. Milosevic transferred the majority of JNA forces in Bosnia to the Serb Republic, which then became the core of the Army of the Republic of Serbia. Milosevic appointed General Ratko Mladic to command the Army of the Republic of Serbia which now consisted of approximately 80,000 troops. Noel Malcolm argues that these changes were merely cosmetic and that the Serb chain of command still ran back

---

[142]Malcolm, 230-231.

[143]David Rohde, *End Game: The Betrayal and Fall of Srebrenica, Europe's Worst Massacre Since WWII* (Boulder, CO: Westview Press, 1998), Ch 1.

53

to Milosevic.[144] In Bosnia, the Serbs had about 300 tanks, 200 armored personnel carriers, 80 artillery pieces, and 40 aircraft.[145] Thus the Serbs had the largest, best organized and equipped force within the former Yugoslavia, with a significant advantage with respect to armor, artillery, and heavy weapons.

These regular forces were supported by paramilitary groups such as Arkan's Tigers, Seselj's Cetniks, and Jovic's White Eagles.[146] Serb paramilitary groups had been in operation in Croatia since 1990.[147] In 1991 the Ministry of the Interior of Belgrade established a training camp for the then "Serbian Volunteer Guard" which was commanded by Željko Ražnjatović, also known as Arkan of Arkan's Tigers.[148] This combination of regular forces, paramilitary, and arming segments of the population gave the Serbs a significant military advantage which was maintained by the UN arms embargo.[149]

The main Bosnian Muslim force was the BiH. The BiH spawned largely from the JNA Territorial Defense Force and was comprised of Light Infantry reservists.[150] BiH Brigades were usually drawn from the same town with the mayor often serving as the Commander.[151] In 1991, the heavily Serb JNA removed much of the Territorial Defense Force's weapons leaving the Territorial Defense Forces in a position of relative weakness when war broke out in 1992.[152] While the BiH may have only had an estimated two tanks and two Armored Personnel Carriers in

---

[144]Noel Malcolm, *Bosnia: A Short History* (New York University Press, 1996), 238.

[145]Malcolm, 243.

[146]Ibid., 226, 236, 238.

[147]Ibid., 226.

[148]Ibid.

[149]Ibid., 243.

[150]Michael J. Fallon, "The United Nations Protection Force's Effectiveness in Bosnia: Campaign Planning and Peacekeeping" (Master's Thesis, Command and General Staff College, Fort Leavenworth, 1996), 55.

[151]Ibid., 57.

[152]Ibid.

September 1992, they had some success in growing their heavy forces by capturing equipment.[153] In June 1993 they had about 40 tanks and 30 Armored Personnel Carriers which grew to an estimated 85 tanks, 130 Armored Personnel Carriers, and 300 artillery pieces by September 1993.[154] While the BiH grew to be substantial in troop numbers, 110,000, it was continually hampered by a relative lack of armor and artillery.

The Croats in western Bosnia were initially more prepared for the coming fight than their Bosnian Muslim counterparts. The Croatian Defense Council (HVO) grew from a mix of local defenders and Croatian Paramilitary.[155] The Croatian Paramilitary were officially integrated into the Croatian Army during their fight for independence with 5,000 of them later comprising a significant portion of the newly formed HVO that totaled 15,000.[156] However, the HVO differed significantly from the BiH, in that it received routine support and cooperation from the military of Croatia. This was crucial, especially with respect to heavy weapons. The HVO often would either borrow Croatian Armor and Artillery or be supported by it. Additionally, Croatian officers were loaned to the HVO, forming most of its higher level leadership. Men and material went back and forth between the HVO and Croatian Military so frequently that soldiers routinely wore Velcro unit patches that they would swap out, depending upon which command they were operating under. While the HVO was relatively smaller in overall numbers, Croatian reinforcement of officers and heavy equipment leveled the playing field.

Character of Intervention Force

The UNPROFOR was beset by turmoil due to its frequent change in mission and composition almost immediately. UNPROFOR would grow from a hastily deployed group of 75

---

[153]Malcolm, 243.

[154]Malcolm, 243; Fallon 57.

[155]Malcolm, 240.

[156]Ibid.

observers to maintain a tenuous cease-fire in Croatia in April 1992, to reopening the airport in Sarajevo, protecting safe areas, protecting humanitarian aid convoys, eventually growing to almost 37,915 troops in Croatia, Bosnia, and Macedonia in March 1995.[157] UNPROFOR was a small force that was lightly equipped for what was envisioned as a peacekeeping operation and nearly devoid of tanks and artillery.

Force Ratios

As mentioned in the literature review, force to population ratios is widely considered useful analytically, can be calculated numerous ways with one way being to compare the size of the population to the intervention force. Bosnia is believed to have had a prewar population of approximately 4.2 million. The size of UNPROFOR changed over time as the organization and mandate grew. What started as a force of 4 Battalions, grew to contain 7,000 soldiers by August of 1991. Resolutions in 1994 increased UNPROFOR to 17,600. UNPROFOR then proceeded to grow incrementally as the UN authorized more forces, until reaching peak strength of 37, 915 soldiers from 37 countries spread amongst Bosnia, Croatia, and Macedonia in March of 1995. By mid 1994, the ratio of UNPROFR to members of the populations was approximately 4.19 peacekeepers per 1,000 Bosnian. At its peak 21,590, ratio of UNPROFOR to population was approximately 5.14 peacekeepers per 1,000 Bosnians.

Relative force ratios were also dismally low and not in UNPROFOR's favor with respect to warring factions of the Serb Bosnian Serb Army (BSA), Bosnian BiH, and Croat HVO. Not only was UNPROFOR relatively weak numerically, they also lacked armored forces, heavy weapons, and artillery. Relative force ratios between the Croat HVO and UNPROFOR were about 1:1.12, though the HVO had a marked advantage with respect to heavy weapons. The Serb BSA enjoyed a numerical advantage of either 3.24 or 3.70:1 over UNPROFOR, depending upon

---

[157]General Accountability Office, 44.

which source you use for the size of the BSA. The Bosnian BiH grew into the largest force due to its large reserve forces, resulting in a numeric advantage of 5.09:1 over UNPROFOR. The only real advantage in arms held by UNPROFOR was NATO's air power in the region which supported UNPROFOR but was not assigned to UNPROFOR's command. Yet this relative advantage in air power often remained not used for various reasons at various times. UNPROFOR was expected to hold at bay, either peacekeeping or enforcing, an aggregate force of belligerents that outnumbered it somewhere between 6.91 or 9.69:1.

Table 3.   Force Ratios in Bosnia

	Number of Troops	UNPROFOR in Bosnia	Ratio
BSA	70,000	21,590	3.24:1
BSA	80,000	21,590	3.70:1
BiH Active	60,000	21,590	2.77:1
BiH + Armed Reserves	110,000	21,590	5.09:1
HVO	19,200	21,590	1:1.1
Low Total Estimate	149,200	21,590	6.91:1
High Total Estimate	209,200	21,590	9.69:1
Population in Bosnia	4.2 million	21,590	5.14 per 1000

Source: Created by author.

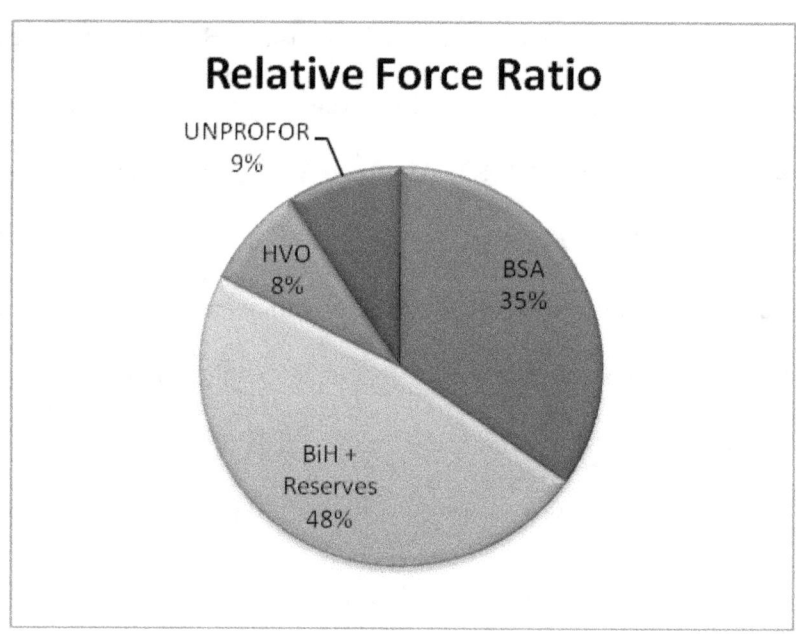

Figure 2.   Force Ratios in Bosnia

Source: Created by author.

Examining UNPROFOR's force ratios, combat power relative to the population and the

belligerent armies, it is revealed that they were significantly under resourced to accomplish their

mandate. With respect to the population, UNPROFORs ratio of 4.19 which grew to 5.14 fell well

short of the 13.26 per 1000 suggested by Mark MacGrath's work. In fact, UNPROFOR's

manning during the early years of the operation just met the level of police to population in the

US at 4.1 per 1,000. However, the US Police Force is not charged with keeping the peace during

a civil war against multiple factions that have standing armies equipped with tanks, heavy

weapons, and artillery. UNPROFOR's amount of combat power also fell below doctrinal

planning rule of thumb that recommends the defending force have at least a ratio of 1:3 and

conversely 3:1 when attacking. With UNPROFOR's estimated ratio ranging from a high estimate,

best case, of 1:6.91 or the low estimate of 1:9.69 placed it in a position where it could not be

expected to defend itself, never mind protect the population or enforce its mandate. The fact that

UNPROFOR had been dispersed through the country's urban and rough terrain, lacked heavy forces, and was reluctant to exploit its air power advantage only magnified their relative weakness.

C2 Structure

The UNPROFOR Headquarters was divided into three echelons that can be described as strategic, operational, and tactical. The policy level headquarters were with the UN Secretary-General, at the UN Headquarters in New York and the UN High Commissioner for Refugees in Geneva. Both of these organizations provided guidance to the UNPROFOR Headquarters in Zagreb. The operational level had four distinct headquarters: the Division of Management and Administration, the Force Commander, the Civil Affairs Office, and the local UN High Commissioner for Refugees Headquarters in Zagreb. In theory, the military chain of command ran from the UN Secretary-General and UN High Commissioner for Refugees to the UNPROFOR Headquarters, to the Force Commander, out to the tactical level commanders, i.e. Bosnia Herzegovina Command. However, the organizational diagram belies the ad hoc, multinational composition of these headquarters.

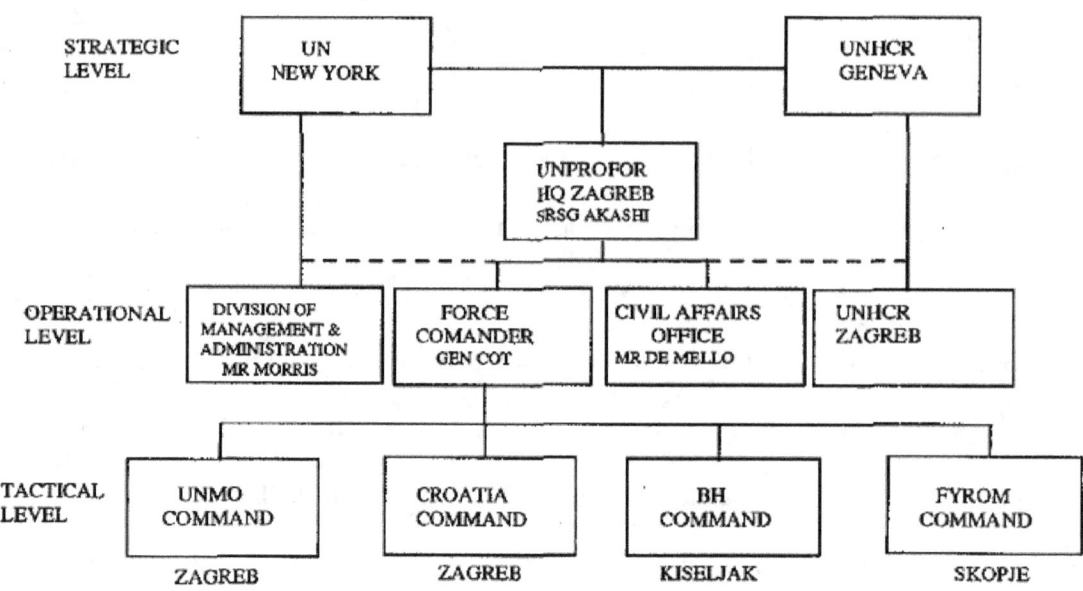

UNPROFOR FEBRUARY 1994

Figure 3.   United Nations Protection Forces Organization

Source: Michael J. Fallon, "The United Nations Protection Force's Effectiveness in Bosnia: Campaign Planning and Peacekeeping" (Master's Thesis, Command and General Staff College, Fort Leavenworth, KS, 1996), 93.

Throughout the chain of command, there were disagreements about what should be done and how to do it. These disagreements resulted from the various actors' different roles, different opinions, personalities, and national agendas. For example, many ground commanders and their governments resisted increase use of air strikes, fearing that the heavily armed belligerents would retaliate against their lightly armed small formations, and instead preferred to negotiate with the belligerents to gain security. Conversely, the US, who did not initially contribute ground forces, advocated through NATO for an increase of air power.[158] Not only did these and similar

---

[158]Trevor Findlay, *Use of Force in UN Peace Operations* (Oxford: Oxford University Press, 2002), 234-236.

disagreements create fiction and limit action, they often resulted in the commander's on the

ground requests for air support to be cancelled by either his military or civilian superiors.[159]

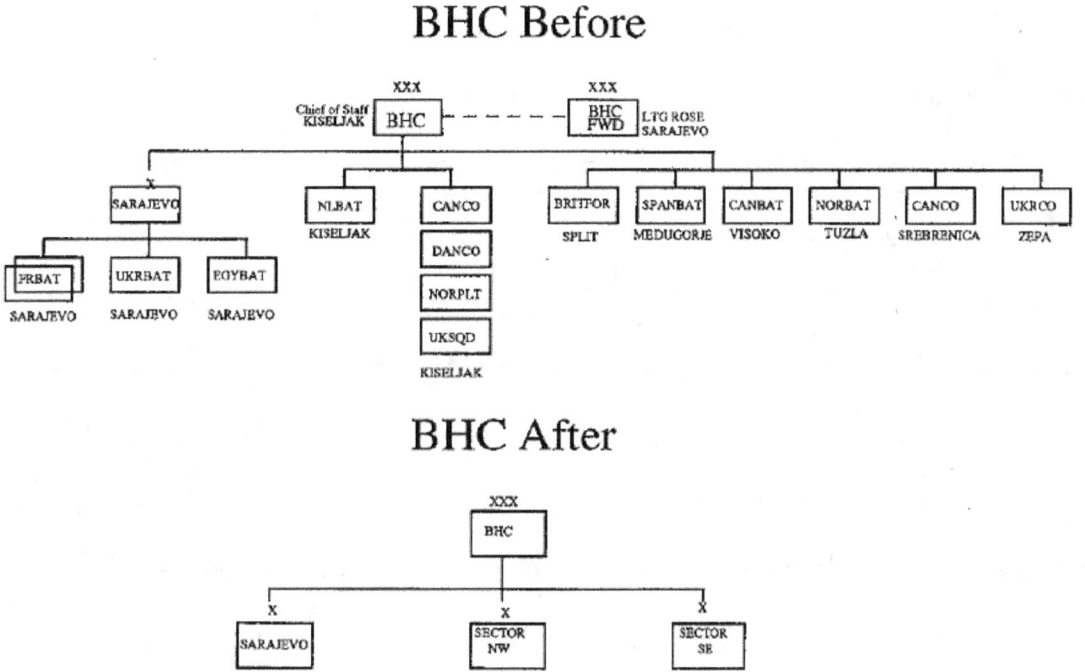

Figure 4.   UNPROFOR Organizational Integration Over Time

Source: Michael J. Fallon, "The United Nations Protection Force's Effectiveness in Bosnia: Campaign Planning and Peacekeeping" (Master's Thesis, Command and General Staff College, Fort Leavenworth, 1996), 92.

Composite Mandate

The following is a composite mandate consisting of key components of the mission

handed down from the UNSC. It shows when key objectives, missions, or powers were granted or

assigned to UNPROFOR followed by the resolution number and date. The list is not exhaustive

---

[159]Findlay, *Use of Force*, 235.

and does not include every element of all the resolutions but it does depict the broad mandate that

UNPROFOR operated under. It is organized chronologically by year.

In 1991 there were three UNSCRs concerning the former Yugoslavia. The first key

resolution enacted an arms embargo throughout the former Yugoslavia.[160] Two more resolutions

followed calling for full compliance with the Geneva ceasefire agreement for Croatia[161] and the

dispatching of a small group of personnel to Croatia.[162]

Overall, there were 26 Security Council resolutions regarding the former Yugoslavia in

1992. Early in the year, the resolutions focused on Croatia since that is where the majority of

fighting was occurring. The Security Council responded by deploying 50 liaison officers, later

increasing the amount of liaison officers, and established and deployed UNPROFOR.[163] As the

resolutions then began to reflect, the fighting had shifted from Croatia to Bosnia with the

sanctioning of Serbia and Montenegro. The UNSC then authorized the UNPROFOR deployment

to Sarajevo and later authorized additional UNPROFOR deployments to Sarajevo, with the

---

[160]United Nations, Security Council Resolution 713, *Arms Embargo, Applying to (former) Yugoslavia*, 3009th Meeting, September 25, 1991, http://www.nato.int/ifor/un/u910925a.htm (accessed November 17, 2012).

[161]United Nations, Security Council Resolution 721, *Full Compliance with Geneva Ceasefire Agreement (Croatia)*, 3018th Meeting, November 27, 1991, http://www.nato.int/ifor/un/u911127a.htm (accessed November 17, 2012).

[162]United Nations, Security Council Resolution 724, *Dispatch of Small Group of Personnel (Croatia); Mandate UN Sanctions Cmt*, 3023rd Meeting, December 15, 1991, http://www.nato.int/ifor/un/u911215a.htm (accessed November 17, 2012).

[163]United Nations, Security Council Resolution 727, *Dispatch of 50 Military Liaison Officers (Croatia)*, 3023th Meeting, January 8, 1992, http://www.nato.int/ifor/un/u920108a.htm (accessed November 17, 2012): United Nations, Security Council Resolution 740, *Approval Peacekeeping Plan; Increasing Military Liaison Officers to 75*, 3049th Meeting, February 7, 1992, http://www.nato.int/ifor/un/u920207a.htm (accessed November 17, 2012); United Nations, Security Council Resolution 743, *Establishment of UNPROFOR (Croatia) for Initial 12 Month Period*, 3055th Meeting, February 21, 1992, http://www.nato.int/ifor/un/u920221a.htm (accessed November 17, 2012); United Nations, Security Council Resolution 749, *Authorization for Full Deployment of UNPROFOR in UNPA's (Croatia)*, 3066th Meeting, April 7, 1992, http://www.nato.int/ifor/un/u920407a.htm (accessed November 17, 2012).

mandate to ensure security of the airport.[164] Less than two weeks later more reinforcements of

UNPROFOR in Sarajevo were authorized. By August and September the mandate had expanded

asking states facilitate delivery of humanitarian aid, demanded unimpeded access for

humanitarian organizations, and eventually tasked UNPROFOR to protect humanitarian convoys

in Bosnia.[165] The last military significant resolution for UNPROFOR in 1992 was the

establishment of the no fly zone over Bosnia, which Security Council tasked UNPROFOR to

monitor and authorize all flights within.[166]

Not only did 1993 have the most security resolutions, with respect to former Yugoslavia,

36, it also contained some of the most controversial. In response to increased aggression against

UNPROFOR, the Security Council demanded the cessation of attacks against UNPROFOR, an

end to violations of the cease-fire agreement, and respect for UNPROFOR's security.[167]

UNPROFOR was also authorized to enforce the no fly zone that they were tasked with

---

[164]United Nations, Security Council Resolution 758, *UNPROFOR Mandate Enlarged for Re-opening Sarajevo Airport*, 3083rd Meeting, June 8, 1992, http://www.nato.int/ifor/un/ u920608a.htm (accessed November 17, 2012); United Nations, Security Council Resolution 761, *Authorization De-ployment UNPROFOR Sarajevo Airport/Delivery Humanitarian Aid*, 3087th Meeting, June 29, 1992, http://www.nato.int/ifor/un/u920629a.htm (accessed November 17, 2012).

[165]United Nations, Security Council Resolution 770, *Delivery of Humanitarian Aid and Access to Camps, etc. (BH)*, 3106th Meeting, August 13, 1992, http://www.nato.int/ifor/un/u920813a.htm (accessed November 17, 2012): United Nations, Security Council Resolution 776, *UNPROFOR Mandate Enlarged to Protect Relief Convoys in BH*, 3114th Meeting, September 14, 1992, http://www.nato.int/ifor/un/u920914a.htm (accessed November 17, 2012).

[166]United Nations, Security Council Resolution 781, *Establishment of No-Fly Zone over Bosnia-Herzegovina*, 3122nd Meeting, October 9, 1992, http://www.nato.int/ifor/un/u921009a. htm (accessed November 17, 2012); United Nations, Security Council Resolution 786, *Monitoring NFZ, Including Deployment of 75 UNMOs on Airfields*, 3133rd Meeting, November 10, 1992, http://www.nato.int/ifor/un/u921110a.htm (accessed November 17, 2012).

[167]United Nations, Security Council Resolution 802, *Cessation of Croation Offensive (UNPA South) & Safety UN Personnel*, January 25, 1993, http://www.nato.int/ifor/un/ u930125a.htm (accessed November 17, 2012).

monitoring six months ago.[168] Resolution 819 established Srebrenica as safe area and would later

prove to be controversial.[169] Later six additional safe areas were added within Bosnia and

approximately a month later the UNPROFOR mandate was enlarged to deter attacks on safe

areas.[170] Later in June, the Security Council authorized additional reinforcement of UNPROFOR

and extended their mandate.[171] The last significant resolution in 1993 was the UN call for a cease-

fire in Bosnia.[172]

The Security Council Resolutions in 1994 made almost no changes to the UNPROFOR

mandate. The resolutions were less numerous and significant in 1994, yet they reflect a

significant change in tone and attitude. First, a Special Coordinator was appointed for Sarajevo in

March.[173] UNPROFOR personnel were again increased, this time by 6,550 and their mandate was

extended.[174] Additionally, the Security Council demanded the immediate release of UN personnel

---

[168]United Nations, Security Council Resolution 816, *Extending No-Fly Zone Bosnia-Herzegovina (Enforcement)*, 3192nd Meeting, March 31, 1993, http://www.nato.int/ifor/un/u930331a.htm (accessed November 17, 2012).

[169]United Nations, Security Council Resolution 819, *Srebrenica Declared "Safe Area,"* 3199th Meeting, April 16, 1993, http://www.nato.int/ifor/un/u930416a.htm (accessed November 17, 2012).

[170]United Nations, Security Council Resolution 824, *Sarajevo, Tuzla, Bihac, Gorazde, Zepa, & Srebrenica "Safe Areas,"* 3208th Meeting, May 6, 1993, http://www.nato.int/ifor/un/u930506a.htm (accessed November 17, 2012).

[171]United Nations, Security Council Resolution 844, *Authorization for 7,600 Troops for "Safe Areas" and use of Air Power*, 3241st Meeting, June 18, 1993, http://www.nato.int/ifor/un/u930618c.htm (accessed November 17, 2012).

[172]United Nations, Security Council Resolution 871, *Extension of UNPROFOR Mandate until 31 March 1994*, 3286th Meeting, October 4, 1993, http://www.nato.int/ifor/un/u931004a.htm (accessed November 17, 2012).

[173]United Nations, Security Council Resolution 877, *Appointment Mr. Escovar-Salem as Prosecutor Inter-National Tribunal*, 3296th Meeting, October 21, 1993, http://www.nato.int/ifor/un/u931021a.htm (accessed November 17, 2012).

[174]United Nations, Security Council Resolution 914, *Authorization for Increase UNPROFOR Strength with 6,500 Troops*, 3369th Meeting, April 27, 1994, http://www.nato.int/ifor/un/u940427a.htm (accessed November 17, 2012).

and condemned Serb ethnic cleansing.[175] Resolution 959 required the strengthening of the safe areas Bihac and Sarajevo.[176]

1995 saw significant resolutions for the UNSC. The first major change was that they authorized another 12,500 troops for UNPROFOR, who would come from NATO's Rapid Reaction Force with UNSCR 998.[177] The Security Council also tasked restoration of safe area Srebrenica, UNSCR 1004, and phased lifting of the arms embargo, UNSCR 1019.[178] Finally, the UN largely turned the mission in Bosnia over to NATO on December 15, 1995 with UNSCR 1031 and its authorization of the Implementation Force.[179]

As Steven Findlay points out, the UNSCR had authorized two separate organizations, UNPROFOR and NATO, to use force on the UNSCR's behalf, with different means, in varying domains, and obliged them to cooperate and coordinate with each other.[180] However, one could argue that the ambiguity surrounding this arrangement reflected an UNSCR assumption that UNPROFOR and NATO could and would cooperate. The desired cooperation proved harder in practice. This ad hoc cooperation evolved into what became known as the dual-key system.

---

[175]United Nations, Security Council Resolution 913, *Ceasefire and Withdrawal of Forces from Gorazde*. 3367th Meeting. April 22, 1994. http://www.nato.int/ifor/un/u940422a.htm (accessed November 17, 2012); United Nations, Security Council Resolution 941, *Condemnation of "Ethnic Cleansing" by the Bosnian Serbs*, 3428th Meeting, September 23, 1994, http://www.nato.int/ifor/un/u940923a.htm (accessed November 17, 2012).

[176]United Nations, Security Council Resolution 959, *Strengthening "Safe Areas" Bihac and Sarajevo*, 3462nd Meeting, November 19, 1994, http://www.nato.int/ifor/un/u941119b.htm (accessed November 17, 2012).

[177]United Nations, Security Council Resolution 998, *Authorizing 12,500 Extra UNPF / UNPROFOR Troops (Rapid Reaction Force)*, 3543rd Meeting, June 16, 1995, http://www.nato.int/ifor/un/u950616a.htm (accessed November 17, 2012).

[178]United Nations, Security Council Resolution 1019, *Condemnation of Violations of International Humanitarian Law*, 3591st Meeting, November 9, 1995, http://www.nato.int/ifor/un/u951109a.htm (accessed November 17, 2012).

[179]United Nations, Security Council Resolution 1031, *Authorization of IFOR; Endorsement of HR (Mr. Bildt); Interim CivPol*, 3607th Meeting, December 15, 1995, http://www.nato.int/ifor/un/u951215a.htm (accessed November 17, 2012).

[180]Findlay, 219.

Additionally, the mandate also resulted in a peacekeeping force that was deployed without a peace agreement to keep, was outnumbered and outgunned by the belligerents, and would be forced to rely on airpower for protection and to counter heavy attacks. Unfortunately, unwillingness and inefficient coordination resulted in very little use of airpower when it was requested.

UNPROFOR and NATO developed what became known as the dual-key system as an ad hoc arrangement to approve or deny requests for the use of air support. This system allowed either organization to veto or cancel a mission. Over time the criteria used to decide whether or not a mission was approved became so restrictive that virtually all requests for close air support were denied.[181] This general unwillingness to attack from the air manifested itself on the battlefield with NATO aircraft primarily conducting show of force missions and demonstrations. These tactics were initially successful however; over time air power was no longer a credible threat. This emboldened the Serbs, they would ignore aircraft and believed they could maneuver with impunity. This later proved catastrophic.

Description of Fighting and the Results of

Bosnia's declaration of independence on April 5, 1992 was followed by the declaration of the Federal Republic of Serbia, on April 27, 1992.[182] The European Community not only recognized Bosnia's independence but demanded that the JNA withdraw from Bosnia. While approximately 20,000 members of the JNA did withdraw, an estimated 80,000 remained and formed the core of the newly established Army of the Republika Srpska.[183] Serbia then embarked on a strategy of uniting the Serbs within Bosnia, largely by attempting to force Bosnian Muslims

---

[181]Ibid., 235-236.

[182]Robert F. Baumann, George W. Gawrych, and Walter E. Kretchik, *Armed Peacekeeping in Bosnia* (Fort Leavenworth, KS: Combat Studies Institute Press, 2004), 25.

[183]Ibid.

and Croats to flee.[184] Mass killing, that was often referred to as ethnic cleansing, did not seek to eradicate particular ethnicity but was focused on gaining territory. The dominant Serb tactic was to lay siege to a particular town with conventional forces and would also shell the town with artillery. The siege was often followed by paramilitary forces who would ethnically cleanse the town by attacking and kill the local civilians and defenses of a particular ethnicity of those who had remained. The Serbs were the first to employ this strategy, but it would later be adopted and adapted by others in Bosnia.

No particular ethnic group was truly innocent with atrocities committed by all sides.[185] This enabled and further fueled competition over the narrative of who were the "bad guys." Many argued that the Serbs were the main belligerents and had caused the most atrocities.[186] This view was also held by much of the US media and US forces that later deployed as part of the Implementation Force.[187] However, these views contrasts with Taylor's work which can be categorized as sympathetic to the Serbs.[188] Taylor's view is informed by his own experiences as a reporter covering the Canadian contingent, whose sector saw Serbs victimized. The civil war in Bosnia was complex, making it difficult to assign blame to any particular group.

Yet, while no group was innocent, it is reasonable to assign a significant blame against the Serbs. The early Serbian offensives in Bosnia in reaction to Bosnia's independence greatly escalated the conflict and left the Serbs in control of much of the territory. Serbian paramilitary forces, such as the Arkan Tigers, were responsible for a significant portion of the mass killings

---

[184]Ibid.

[185]Ibid, 27.

[186]Malcolm.

[187]Ibid.

[188]Taylor.

committed.[189] By the war's end, all parties had blood on their hands; however, the Serbs had seized the most territory and created the most refugees.[190]

Military effectiveness improved following the catastrophe at Srebrenica and lesser Serb attacks on safe areas at Zepa and Bihac resulted in a decision to streamline the decision approval process to use force and a more aggressive NATO stance.[191] The previous dual-key system of decision-making was streamlined, shifting more authority to NATO commanders.[192]The combination of the ability of to make faster military decisions, resources, and willingness to employ those resources, manifested itself in a NATO air campaign against the Serbs.[193] The NATO air campaign lasted nearly two weeks, consisted of over 3,000 sorties largely against Serb air defense systems and ammunition stores, and forced the Serb commander, Ratko Mladić, to comply by withdrawing most of his heavy weaponry from the exclusion zone around Sarajevo.[194] At the same time, there were successful ground offenses in northwestern Bosnia by Croatian and Bosnian Government forces. While the NATO air campaign did not directly support the ground attach against Serbian forces, since it was heavily focused on air defense targets, it produced indirect benefits by damaging Serbian morale, communications, and logistics capabilities.[195] The balance of military power between the combatants had significantly swung away from Serbian forces. In this instance, transitioning the military lead from an ad hoc UN led coalition, to a standing military alliance in NATO, increased effectiveness and efficiency.

---

[189]Malcolm, 252.

[190]Baumann, Gawrych, and Kretchik, 27.

[191]Malcolm, 264-266.

[192]Ibid., 266.

[193]Ibid.

[194]Ibid.

[195]Malcolm, 266-267.

Broad Analysis

UNPROFOR's effectiveness resulted from a combination of structural and psychological issues. In actuality, UNPROFOR's mission should have been peace enforcement, due to the lack of a peace agreement and the fact all sides were intent on continuing fighting. Yet, UNPROFOR was not resourced with enough combat power, especially with respect to land forces, to coerce the belligerents to cease fighting. The resources and mandate did not match the situation on the ground.

Additionally, with the UNPROFOR and NATO both authorized to use force in the same theater it resulted in a dual-key approval system for the use of air power, that generally resulted in mission requests being denied by default. This greatly reduced the ability for air power to deter and influence the situation on the ground.

The last major impediment to UNPROFOR's success was a general lack of will to fight, which in many ways stemmed from the perception that they were peacekeeping and should not use their arms to enforce the peace. If the idea of peace enforcement were widely embraced, air power could have been used to reinforce the small, lightly equipped ground forces. Much of UNPROFOR's leadership seemed determined to not fight.

Theses analytic conclusions are supported by the events that unfolded once a credible, determined force, NATO's Implementation Force, assumed the mission from UNPROFOR. Once the decision was made to truly pick a side, and employ force to determine the outcome, NATO was able to beat the Serbian forces back and all belligerent parties quickly minimized the amount of fighting.

Sadly, this decision and willingness to act only came after many civilian deaths and tragedies such as Srebrenica.

Battle Analysis: Srebrenica

The town of Srebrenica was the original UN safe area and was originally informally placed under UN protection when the French General Philippe Morillon declared it so, and raised the UN flag over the town in 1993. Later the UNSC codified this protection when it declared Srebrenica as safe area in Resolution 819. In 1995 UNPROFOR was protecting the town with 300 lightly armed Dutch Soldiers. They were armed with small arms, mortars, anti-tank missiles, and had Armored Personnel Carriers mounted with machine guns. Unlike the nearby Serbian forces, the Dutch did not have any tanks or artillery with them.

On July 6, 1995 Serbs began preparing from positions south of Dutch UN observation posts that guarded the Southern approach to the town. The Bosnian Serbs begin their attack in earnest on July 8, 1995 with its tanks and artillery forcing the Dutch to withdraw from the southern observation posts.[196] The Dutch request air support but none appears. On July 10, the Dutch attempted to establish new blocking positions with the limited combat power available to them, knowing that the viability of their positions rest solely on close air support from NATO. While not coordinated, the Bosnian Muslims launch a counter attack. Bosnian Muslim irregular infantry sneak up and ambush the Serb tanks with rocket propelled grenades and small arms forcing them to retreat. However, the Muslims were unable to hold their gains when the Serbs counterattacked with artillery and armor, causing Muslim casualties and forcing their retreat. The Dutch battalions repeated requests for air support continue to be denied. In fact, the Dutch will have six requests for air support denied and only one request filled before the fall of Srebrenica. By July 12 UNPROFOR had surrender Srebrenica to the BSA and the Serbs proceeded to separate an estimated 7,000 Bosnian Muslim men and boys. These Muslims were never seen

---

[196]Rohde, 22.

again and are presumed to have been massacred by the Serbs, with many continuing to blame the Dutch and or UNPROFOR for failing to prevent it.

The fall and subsequent massacre at Srebrenica highlights numerous weaknesses within the multinational coalition. UNPROFOR suffered from an inefficient command and control structure, that was further hampered by the various agendas of the different stakeholders holding key positions. The dual-key system for approving air attacks ultimately prevented the use of airpower, which over time emboldened the Bosnian Serbs to the extent that they confidently attacked Srebrenica with a small force of four tanks and a few hundred infantry.[197] The Dutch forces at Srebrenica suffered from an overall lack of numbers, tanks, and artillery, like most of UNPROFOR, and were overmatched when the BSA decided to attack. Arguably the greatest limitation facing UNPROFOR was a general lack of will to use force in the face of adversaries who did not suffer from the same compunction. Much of UNPROFOR's leadership, both civilian and military, still strove to remain neutral and feared that using force would trigger retribution against their weak forces and humanitarian convoys. Viewed as a whole, the lack of resources, will, and unity of command created the conditions for the tragedy at Srebrenica. A general lack of combat power and inefficient command and control structures put the Dutch forces from UNPROFOR and the town of Srebrenica at risk, however they potentially could have been saved if key leaders had chosen to use the air power available to fend off the BSA attack.

---

[197] Rohde, 354.

Conclusion

Having unity of command, or a lack thereof, is often not significant enough to cause a military intervention to succeed. The problems are so complex and difficult that command and control will rarely be the proximate cause of mission failure. Moreover, while it is still preferable to build an efficient headquarters that enables organizational efficiency, having unity of command is does not necessarily result in a successful operation.

The quantitative analysis shows that interventions on the side of the government during stability operations had no effect on the outcome. The hypothesis that interventions by unilateral actors on the side of the government would be more likely to be successful than coalitions was not supported by the statistical analysis. The additional inefficiencies and friction that result from using a coalition were not sufficient to consistently prevent success.

The case studies highlight that coalition operations are quite complex. The qualitative analysis highlights that numerous factors including command and control negatively affect the outcome of military interventions. The missions in the Congo and Bosnia both had command and control issues and often struggled to produce unity of action. Yet, the case studies show that various other factors were present that appear to have been more pressing and damaging to the overall mission. At times, both missions suffered from a lack of resources and willingness to use force.

The analysis also shows that more study should be done on interventions in general on the side of the government to ascertain why they do not have a consistent effect on the outcome. While the cases examined here highlight numerous commonalities and differences between these two interventions, there is still much work to be done to better understand what factors affect success.

Bibliography

Books

Baumann, Robert, George W. Gawrych, and Walter E. Kretchik. *Armed Peacekeeping in Bosnia*. Fort Leavenworth, KS: Combat Studies Institute Press, 2004.

Boulden, Jane. *Peace Enforcement: The United Nations Experience in Congo, Somalia, and Bosnia*. Westport, CT: Praeger Publishers, 2001.

Collier, Paul, and Nicholas Sambanis, eds. *Understanding Civil War: Evidence and Analysis*. Washington, DC: World Bank Publications, 2005.

Collier, Paul, Anke Hoeffler, and Nicholas Sambanis. "The Collier-Hoeffler Model of Civil War Onset and the Case Study Project Research Design." In *Understanding Civil War: Evidence and Analysis*, edited by Paul Collier, and Nicholas Sambanis, 1-34. Washington, DC: World Bank Publications, 2005.

Connable, Ben, and Martin C. Libicki. *How Insurgencies End*. Santa Monica, CA: RAND Corporation, 2010.

Diehl, Paul. *International Peacekeeping*. Baltimore, MD: The John Hopkins University Press, 1994.

Dobbins, James, John G. McGinn, Keith Crane, Seth G. Jones, Rollie Lal, Andrew Rathmell, Rachel M. Swanger, and Anga Timilsina. *America's Role in Nation-Building: From Germany to Iraq*. Santa Monica, CA: RAND Corporation, 2012.

Dobbins, James, Seth G. Jones, Keith Crane, Andrew Rathmell, Brett Steele, Richard Teltschik, and Anga Timilsina. *The UN's Role in Nation-Building: From the Congo to Iraq*. Santa Monica, CA: RAND Corporation, 2005.

Doyle, Michael W., and Nicholas Sambanis. *Making War and Building Peace*. Princeton, NJ: Princeton University Press, 2006.

Findlay, Trevor. *The Blue Helmets' First War? Use of Force by the UN in the Congo 1960-1964*. Clementsport: Canadian Peacekeeping Press, 1999.

———. *Use of Force in UN Peace Operations*. Oxford: Oxford University Press, 2002.

Guevara, Ernesto "Che". *The African Dream: The Diaries of the Revolutionary War in the Congo*. New York: Grove Press, 2000.

Hart, B.H. Liddell. *Strategy*. New York: Praeger, 1954.

Kalyvas, Stathis N. *The Logic of Violence in Civil Wars*. Cambridge: Cambridge University Press, 2006.

Gordon, King J. *The United Nations in the Congo: A Quest for Peace*. Washington, DC: Carnegie Endowment for International Peace, 1962.

Lefever, Ernest W. *Crisis in the Congo: A United Nations Force in Action*. Washington, DC: Brookings Institute, 1965.

Licklider, Roy, ed. *Stop the Killing How Civil Wars End*. New York: New York University Press, 1993.

Malcolm, Noel. *Bosnia: A Short History*. New York University Press, 1996.

Mandel, Robert. *The Meaning of Military Victory*. Boulder, CO: Lynne Rienner Publications, 2006.

McGrath, John J. *Boots on the Ground: Troop Density in Contingency Operations*. Fort Leavenworth KS: CSI Press, 2006.

Regan, Patrick. *Civil Wars and Foreign Powers: Outside Intervention in Intrastate Conflict*. Ann Arbor, MI: University of Michigan Press, 2002.

Rikhye, Indar Jit. *Military Advisor to the Secretary-General*. New York: St. Martin's Press, 1993.

Rohde, David. *End Game: The Betrayal and Fall of Srebrenica, Europe's Worst Massacre Since WWII*. Boulder, CO: Westview Press, 1998.

Seybolt, Taylor B. *Humanitarian Military Intervention: The Conditions for Success and Failure*. Oxford: Oxford University Press, 2007.

Shelling, Thomas C. *Arms and Influence*. New Haven, CT: Yale University Press, 1966.

Taylor, Scott, and Brian Nolan. *Tested Mettle: Canada's Peacekeepers at War*. Ottawa, Canada: Esprit De Corps Books, 1998.

Van Evera, Stephen. *The Guide to Methods for Students of Political Science*. New York: Cornell University Press, 1997.

Thesis

Fallon, Michael J. "The United Nations Protection Force's Effectiveness In Bosnia: Campaign Planning and Peacekeeping." Master's Thesis, Command and General Staff College, Fort Leavenworth, 1996.

Journals

Fearon, James D., and David D. Laitin. "Ethnicity, Insurgency, and Civil War." *American Political Science Review* 97, no. 1 (February 2003): 75-90.

Krause, Peter J. P. "Troop Levels in Stability Operations: What We Don't Know." *MIT Center for International Studies* (February 2007): 3.

Lockyer, Adam." Foreign Intervention and Warfare in Civil Wars." *Review of International Studies* 37, no. 5 (December 2011): 2337-2364.

Mueller, John. "War Has Almost Ceased to Exist: An Assessment." *Political Science Quarterly* 124 (November 2009): 297-321.

Quinlivan, James T. "Force Requirements in Stability Operations." *Parameters* (Winter 1995): 59-69.

Rice, Anthony J. "Command and Control: The Essence of Coalition Warfare." *Parameters* (Spring 1997): 152.

RisCassi, Robert W. "Principles for Coalition Warfare." *Joint Forces Quarterly* (Summer 1993): 58-71.

Singer, J. David. "Inter-nation Influence: A Formal Model." *The American Political Science Review* 57, no. 2 (June 1963): 420-430.

Government Documents

Department of the Army. ADP 3-0, *Unified Land Operations*. Washington, DC: Government Printing Office, October 2011.

Department of Defense. *Defense Budget Priorities and Choices*. Washington, DC: Government Printing Office, 2012.

Department of State. Bureau of African Affairs. "Background Note: The Democratic Republic of the Congo." http://www.state.gov/r/pa/ei/bgn/2823.htm (accessed July 26, 2012).

Government Accountability Office. GAO/NSIAD-95-148BR, *Update on the Situation in the Former Yugoslavia*. Washington, DC: General Accounting Office, May 1995.

Joint Chiefs of Staff. Joint Publication (JP) 1-0, *Joint Personnel Support*. Washington, DC: Government Printing Office, 2011.

———. Joint Publication (JP) 3-0, Joint Operations. Washington, DC: Government Printing Office, 2011.

———. Joint Publication (JP) 3-16, *Multinational Operations*. Washington, DC: Government Printing Office, 2007.

United Nations. General Assembly. A/RES/60/1, *2005 World Summit Outcome*. 60th Sess. http://www.un.org/summit2005/ (accessed November 14, 2012).

———. Department of Public Information. *Former Yugoslav-UNPROFOR*. September 1996. http://www.un.org/Depts/DPKO/Missions/unprof_b.htm (accessed November 17, 2012).

———. Security Council. Resolution 143 (S/4387). *The Congo Question*. July 14, 1960. 873rd meeting.

———. Security Council Resolution 145 (S/4405). *The Congo Question*. July 22, 1960. 879th meeting.

———. Security Council. Resolution 156 (S/4491). *Question Related to the Dominique Republic.* September 9, 1960. 895th meeting.

———. Security Council. Resolution 161 (S/4741). *The Congo Question.* February 21, 1961.

———. Security Council Resolution 713, *Arms Embargo, Applying to (former) Yugoslavia.* 3009th Meeting. September 25, 1991. http://www.nato.int/ifor/un/u910925a.htm (accessed November 17, 2012).

———. Security Council Resolution 721, *Full Compliance with Geneva Ceasefire Agreement (Croatia).* 3018th. Meeting. November 27, 1991. http://www.nato.int/ifor/un/u911127a.htm (accessed November 17, 2012).

———. Security Council Resolution 724, *Dispatch of Small Group of Personnel (Croatia); Mandate UN Sanctions Cmt.* 3023rd Meeting. December 15, 1991. http://www.nato.int/ifor/un/u911215a.htm (accessed November 17, 2012).

———. Security Council Resolution 727, *Dispatch of 50 Military Liaison Officers (Croatia).* 3023th Meeting. January 8, 1992. http://www.nato.int/ifor/un/u920108a.htm (accessed November 17, 2012).

———. Security Council Resolution 740, *Approval Peacekeeping Plan; Increasing Military Liaison Officers to 75.* 3049th Meeting. February 7, 1992. http://www.nato.int/ifor/un/u920207a.htm (accessed November 17, 2012).

———. Security Council Resolution 743, *Establishment of UNPROFOR (Croatia) for Initial 12 Month Period.* 3055th Meeting. February 21, 1992. http://www.nato.int/ifor/un/u920221a.htm (accessed November 17, 2012).

———. Security Council Resolution 749, *Authorization for Full Deployment of UNPROFOR in UNPA's (Croatia).* 3066th Meeting. April 7, 1992. http://www.nato.int/ifor/un/u920407a.htm (accessed November 17, 2012).

———. Security Council Resolution 758, *UNPROFOR Mandate Enlarged for Re-opening Sarajevo Airport.* 3083rd Meeting. June 8, 1992. http://www.nato.int/ifor/un/u920608a.htm (accessed November 17, 2012).

———. Security Council Resolution 761, *Authorization De-ployment UNPROFOR Sarajevo Airport/Delivery Humanitarian Aid.* 3087th Meeting. June 29, 1992. http://www.nato.int/ifor/un/u920629a.htm (accessed November 17, 2012).

———. Security Council Resolution 770, *Delivery of Humanitarian Aid and Access to Camps, etc. (BH).* 3106th Meeting. August 13, 1992. http://www.nato.int/ifor/un/u920813a.htm (accessed November 17, 2012).

———. Security Council Resolution 776, *UNPROFOR Mandate Enlarged to Protect Relief Convoys in BH.* 3114th Meeting. September 14, 1992. http://www.nato.int/ifor/un/u920914a.htm (accessed November 17, 2012).

———. Security Council Resolution 781, *Establishment of No-Fly Zone over Bosnia-Herzegovina*. 3122nd Meeting. October 9, 1992. http://www.nato.int/ifor/un/u921009a.htm (accessed November 17, 2012).

———. Security Council Resolution 786, *Monitoring NFZ, Including Deployment of 75 UNMOs on Airfields*. 3133rd Meeting. November 10, 1992. http://www.nato.int/ifor/un/u921110a.htm (accessed November 17, 2012).

———. Security Council Resolution 802, *Cessation of Croation Offensive (UNPA South) & Safety UN Personnel*. January 25, 1993. http://www.nato.int/ifor/un/u930125a.htm (accessed November 17, 2012).

———. Security Council Resolution 816, *Extending No-Fly Zone Bosnia-Herzegovina (Enforcement)*. 3192nd Meeting. March 31, 1993. http://www.nato.int/ifor/un/u930331a.htm (accessed November 17, 2012).

———. Security Council Resolution 819, *Srebrenica Declared "Safe Area."* 3199th Meeting. April 16, 1993. http://www.nato.int/ifor/un/u930416a.htm (accessed November 17, 2012).

———. Security Council Resolution 824, *Sarajevo, Tuzla, Bihac, Gorazde, Zepa, & Srebrenica "Safe Areas."* 3208th Meeting. May 6, 1993. http://www.nato.int/ifor/un/u930506a.htm (accessed November 17, 2012).

———. Security Council Resolution 844, *Authorization for 7,600 Troops for "Safe Areas" and use of Air Power*. 3241st Meeting. June 18, 1993. http://www.nato.int/ifor/un/u930618c.htm (accessed November 17, 2012).

———. Security Council Resolution 871, *Extension of UNPROFOR Mandate until 31 March 1994*. 3286th Meeting. October 4, 1993. http://www.nato.int/ifor/un/u931004a.htm (accessed November 17, 2012).

———. Security Council Resolution 877, *Appointment Mr. Escovar-Salem as Prosecutor Inter-National Tribunal*. 3296th Meeting. October 21, 1993. http://www.nato.int/ifor/un/u931021a.htm (accessed November 17, 2012).

———. Security Council Resolution 913, *Ceasefire and Withdrawal of Forces from Gorazde*. 3367th Meeting. April 22, 1994. http://www.nato.int/ifor/un/u940422a.htm (accessed November 17, 2012).

———. Security Council Resolution 914, *Authorization for Increase UNPROFOR Strength with 6,500 Troops*. 3369th Meeting. April 27, 1994. http://www.nato.int/ifor/un/u940427a.htm (accessed November 17, 2012).

———. Security Council Resolution 941, *Condemnation of "Ethnic Cleansing" by the Bosnian Serbs*. 3428th Meeting. September 23, 1994. http://www.nato.int/ifor/un/u940923a.htm (accessed November 17, 2012).

———. Security Council Resolution 959, *Strengthening "Safe Areas" Bihac and Sarajevo*. 3462nd Meeting. November 19, 1994. http://www.nato.int/ifor/un/u941119b.htm (accessed November 17, 2012).

————. Security Council Resolution 998, *Authorizing 12,500 Extra UNPF / UNPROFOR Troops (Rapid Reaction Force)*. 3543rd Meeting. June 16, 1995. http://www.nato.int/ifor/un/u950616a.htm (accessed November 17, 2012).

————. Security Council Resolution 1004, *Restoration of Safe Area Srebrenica*. 3553rd Meeting. July 12, 1995. http://www.nato.int/ifor/un/u950712a.htm (accessed November 17, 2012).

————. Security Council Resolution 1019, *Condemnation of Violations of International Humanitarian Law*. 3591st Meeting. November 9, 1995. http://www.nato.int/ifor/un/u951109a.htm (accessed November 17, 2012).

————. Security Council Resolution 1031, *Authorization of IFOR; Endorsement of HR (Mr. Bildt); Interim CivPol*. 3607th Meeting. December 15, 1995. http://www.nato.int/ifor/un/u951215a.htm (accessed November 17, 2012).

————. Security Council Resolutions. http://www.nato.int/ifor/un/un-resol.htm (accessed November 17, 2012).

White House. *National Security Strategy*. Washington, DC: Government Printing Office, 2010.

————. "Statement by the President on Libya." August 22, 2011. http://www.whitehouse.gov/the-press-office/2011/08/22/statement-president-libya (accessed June 12, 2012).